Carlos

Knowing and Experiencing God as Life

WITNESS LEE

Living Stream Ministry
Anaheim, CA • www.lsm.org

First Edition, April 2012.

ISBN 978-0-7363-6124-8

Published by

Living Stream Ministry
2431 W. La Palma Ave., Anaheim, CA 92801 U.S.A.
P. O. Box 2121, Anaheim, CA 92814 U.S.A.

Printed in the United States of America

12 13 14 15 16 17 / 9 8 7 6 5 4 3 2 1

CONTENTS

PREFACE

This book is composed of messages given by Brother Witness Lee in a young people's conference in Hong Kong from late July to early August in 1959. The messages were published in Chinese in *The Ministry of the Word* magazine from 1960 to 1961. Two messages from this conference, which were previously published in *Leading the Young People with the Word and the Spirit* (chapters 13 and 14), are not included in this book.

CHAPTER ONE

LIVING BY THE LORD

Scripture Reading: John 6:57, 63; 14:19-20; Gal. 2:19-20; Phil. 1:20-21

There are several important verses in the Bible that contain the word *live*. For example, John 6:57 says, "As the living Father has sent Me and I live because of the Father, so he who eats Me, he also shall live because of Me." The word *live* is used twice in this verse. The first time is concerning the Lord living because of the Father, and the second time is concerning our living because of the Lord by eating the Lord. In 14:19 the Lord said, "Because I live, you also shall live." The word *live* is used twice here also. The first use speaks of the crucified and resurrected Lord living in the believers, and the other speaks of the believers living by the Lord. In Galatians 2:19-20 Paul says, "I through law have died to law that I might live to God. I am crucified with Christ; and it is no longer I who live, but it is Christ who lives in me." In Philippians 1:21 Paul says, "To me, to live is Christ." In these verses the word *live* is related to the believers.

IMPORTANT WORDS IN THE BIBLE

If we can commit these verses to memory, the Holy Spirit will speak to us and will also shine in us. For two thousand years these words have been buried in the Bible and neglected by God's children. I hope that we can now uncover these words.

These verses are very important. Most brothers and sisters highly regard the more common speaking in the Bible, such as, "Wives, be subject to your own husbands" (Eph. 5:22); "husbands, love your wives" (v. 25); "children, obey your parents" (6:1); and "fathers, do not provoke your children" (v. 4).

Most believers regard these words highly and can recite them. However, these words, though precious, are merely like the "watermelon rind" of the Bible. When we eat watermelon, we do not eat the rind, but we eat the precious part inside. Although the Bible contains many precious words concerning God being life to us, it is regrettable that these words have been neglected by many Christians. Innumerable messages are being given to believers every Lord's Day, but it is not common to hear a message concerning God living within the believers or concerning His desire for the believers to live by His life. Some preachers speak about "living for God," but the word *for* causes us to think that we should do something for God. The Bible does not stress our living for God but our letting God live in us, that is, our living according to God, our living by Him, and our living because of Him.

I hope that we would commit these verses to memory. Please do not think that I am bothersome because I ask you to memorize these verses. People who mine precious gems expend great effort in order to cut through rocks and dig deep in the earth. Hence, it is worthwhile to spend a few days to dig out these verses, which are like diamonds.

THE LORD GIVING US LIFE
SO THAT WE WOULD LIVE BY HIM

The precious words in the Bible speak of the Lord coming to be our life. God's children neglect the matter of life. Some who speak of life give the impression that to believe in the Lord is to receive eternal life in the future. They regard eternal life as the blessing that believers will receive in the future. Others think that to believe in the Lord is to receive a life that never perishes. Based on John 3:16, they say that people are destined to perish but that after they receive eternal life, they will not perish. They link eternal life to salvation from perdition.

It is true that those who have eternal life will not perish, because they have received a life that is eternal and cannot perish. However, the divine life does not merely save us from perishing, nor is it merely a promised blessing for the future. The Lord gives us His life so that we may live by Him today.

This is the central teaching in the New Testament. Many verses in the New Testament show that God's purpose in entering into us as life is not merely to save us from perishing, nor is it for us to enjoy the blessing of eternal life in the future. He intends that we would live by Him today. God has entered into us to be our life; hence, He needs to live in us. He is not waiting to be our life in the future. He has entered into us to be our life today. Hence, from the moment we were saved, we should live by the life of God. We do not receive the divine life merely to be delivered from perdition, nor do we receive this life merely to receive a blessing in the future. These things are supplementary, not primary. The primary matter is that God is in us so that we would live by Him. Now we will consider how to live by the Lord.

HE WHO EATS THE LORD
LIVING BECAUSE OF THE LORD

God as life in us is our nourishment, our power. This power is not outward; it supplies us inwardly. John 6:57 says, "The living Father has sent Me and I live because of the Father." In the original language, the expression *because of* also has the meaning of "by" and "through." When the Lord Jesus was living on the earth as a man, He lived by God the Father and through God the Father. He did not live independent of the Father. He lived in God, and He let God live in Him.

When the Lord Jesus lived on the earth, He was a perfect man, yet He did not live by His human life. He was a man in the flesh, but He had no sin. This is what made Him different from other men; everything else about Him was the same as with other men. He had a human life with a human nature. When He lived on the earth, He always put His human life aside instead of living by His human life. He knew that He was sent by the Father to do the Father's work. Hence, the Lord did not work by His own life but by the life of the Father, who was life in Him. He said to His disciples, "The words that I say to you I do not speak from Myself, but the Father who abides in Me does His works" (14:10). This means that He did not live by His human life but by God who lived in Him as the divine life.

The Lord also said, "As the living Father has sent Me and I live because of the Father, so he who eats Me, he also shall live because of Me" (6:57). The expression *eat the Lord* is very particular, but it should be easy for us to comprehend. To eat is to receive into us the things that can nourish and supply us. We eat breakfast in the morning because without the nourishment and supply from the food, we would not have strength for the day. We cannot survive if we do not receive nourishment over a long period of time. We eat because we need the supply. We do not receive a supply from outward empowering or compelling. In order to receive a supply, we need to take in nutrients by digesting and absorbing food. Then the food will become a supply within us. We often do not sense this kind of supply. Having a particular feeling after we eat indicates that we have a problem with our stomach. Otherwise, we will not feel anything after we eat. When our stomach is functioning normally, we automatically receive a supply from the food that we eat without any particular feeling.

Similarly, we often do not sense the Lord's supply within us. Sometimes we pray when we are weak, hoping that a surge of energy will descend upon us to empower us. This may happen occasionally, but it is not a normal situation. The normal situation is that the Lord supplies us within because we daily receive Him into us as food by digesting and absorbing Him. When He is supplying us, we feel normal; we do not have a particular feeling. However, when we are short of Him, we will sense something. This shows how the Lord supplies us.

Eating is something normal. There is nothing special about eating. However, many Christians prefer to have special things. They say that they should have a special experience like the disciples had in Acts 2:1-4, when there was a sound out of heaven, as a rushing violent wind, and tongues of fire. Sometimes we may need a special experience, but it should not be our normal situation. Our regular and normal situation is that the Lord is food for us to eat Him as our nourishment. Eating a meal is very ordinary. Since the day that we were born, we have eaten meals daily. We should not focus our attention on special experiences. The more intimate we are with the Lord, the more normal our situation should be, and our experience of the Lord should also be more ordinary. We may have rich or deep experiences, but our situation should be ordinary, because the Lord gives Himself to us as food without much fanfare or special feelings. It is normal to eat bread or to drink milk. When our experience of the Lord is ordinary and normal, it will also be spontaneous and proper. We should not pursue experiences that are out of the ordinary.

EATING THE LORD AND LIVING BY HIM

The Lord Being in the Spirit and in the Word

In order to eat the Lord, we must know where He is. If we desire to eat some food, we need to know where it is located. When we want to eat a meal, we should go to the dining table, because the food is put on the dining table. Where should we go when we have the desire to eat the Lord? The Lord is the Word (John 1:1), and He is also the Spirit (1 Cor. 15:45; 2 Cor. 3:17). Hence, we can say that the Lord is in the Word and also in the Spirit. He is always in His Word and the Spirit. When we use our spirit to contact the Word, the Spirit will touch our spirit. The Spirit and the Word cannot be separated: "The words which I have spoken to you are spirit and are life" (John 6:63). Whenever His words touch our inner being, they become spirit and life. Not only so, the Spirit has entered into us. Hence, the Lord is in the Word and in the Spirit, and the Spirit is in our spirit. Whenever we want to contact the Lord and take Him into us, we can find Him in a definite place. We can find Him in the Bible and in the Spirit. Whenever we desire to receive the Lord, we need to turn to our spirit and also to open the Bible. This is the reason that we need to pray and to read the Bible daily. To pray is to turn to our spirit, and to read the Bible is to contact the Lord's word.

Eating the Lord through Prayer

Some believers do not turn to their spirit when they pray. Some believers pray according to their mind and their preference, and they do not touch their spirit. Such believers pray in the outer man; they do not turn to their spirit in order to pray. As a result, it is difficult for them to touch the Lord.

When we pray, we must turn away from outward things to our spirit. We close our eyes when we pray in order to stop our person. We do not want to turn to the outward things, nor do we want the outward things to distract our inner being. When we turn to our spirit in order to touch God, our prayer will not follow our thoughts or emotions; rather, our prayer will follow the sense in our spirit. Then as we pray one sentence at a time, we will touch God, and our prayer will be solid. This is the way to absorb the Lord.

Eating the Lord through Reading the Bible

It is also easy to touch the Lord when we turn to our spirit and read His Word. Even if we do not understand some words, we can still touch the Lord in our spirit. We might forget what we read, but the Lord has entered into us. Sometimes we are touched by a word or a phrase. We might not understand the words, but we sense that they are precious, and we receive them. These words convey the Lord and His riches to us. When we receive these words, we also receive the Spirit.

Eating the Lord to Live and to Grow

When we pray and read the Word in this way, we will feel satisfied within, just as if we have eaten a meal. Prayer is to contact the Lord, and reading the Word is also to contact the Lord. When we contact Him through prayer and reading the Word, we receive Him. When an electric stove is plugged into an electrical outlet, electricity will immediately flow into the stove. After five minutes the stove will become red hot because of electrical heat. The electric stove is contacting and absorbing electricity. Similarly, when we pray and read the Bible, we contact and absorb the Lord. We eat the Lord by absorbing Him.

When we eat the Lord, His element will increase within us. As long as we will spend a little time in the morning, during the day, and in the evening to turn to our spirit and pray or read the Bible, we will touch, contact, and eat the Lord. What we receive will become our inner supply, our bread of life. It is by and through this inner supply of the bread of life that we can live on the earth.

A good example is an electric fan, which turns continuously by means of an electric current. When we switch off the fan, electricity cannot flow in, and the fan will stop turning. This is an example of how we can live before God. If we contact the Lord, absorb Him, receive Him, and allow Him to enter into us to be our life supply, we will be able to live by Him and express Him.

In order to live in Him, we must daily spend time to turn to our spirit and to read the Word. We can spend ten minutes, twenty minutes, or even better, thirty minutes to read the Word. We must find some time to spend before the Lord. He is in the Word and also in the Spirit. When we touch the Spirit and touch the Word, we touch the Lord. The more we contact Him, the more we will absorb Him and the more we will receive an inward supply, because He is our nourishment. Just as we live and grow by eating food, when we take the Lord as our nourishment, daily we will live by Him and also grow.

John 6:57 and 63 speak of the same thing. In verse 57 the Lord Jesus said, "He who eats Me, he also shall live because of Me." The disciples did not understand this word. Therefore, in verse 63 the Lord Jesus said, "It is the Spirit who gives life…the words which I have spoken to you are spirit and are life." The Lord is in His words, and He is in the Spirit so that we can receive Him. To receive the Lord in His words and in the Spirit is to eat Him.

LIVING BECAUSE THE LORD LIVES

In John 14:19 the Lord said, "Because I live, you also shall live." This refers to the Lord Jesus living in us through His resurrection. The Lord's death was His going, and His resurrection was His coming. In His death the Lord left the disciples, but in His resurrection He entered into the disciples. Hence, we who believe into Him also live, because He has entered into us and is living in us. For this reason, in verse 20 the Lord said, "In that day you will know that I am in My Father, and you in Me, and I in you." This verse is concerning the union between the Lord and us. In order to live before the Lord and to allow Him to be life in us, we should not only turn to our spirit in order to contact and eat Him through His Word; we also need to maintain the condition of being joined to Him. No matter what we are doing, we must be in the Lord and He must be in us.

According to our experience, we are often not in the Lord when we do something or when we speak. It seems as though we leave Him or that He leaves us. Such a feeling is a warning, telling us that our condition is not right. Hence, we must quickly correct our situation and restore our condition; we must restore our experiential union with Him. We should be able to say, "It is the Lord doing this with me, and it is the Lord speaking with me." If we can live in this condition every day, we will be those who take Christ as life and live by Him.

Chapter Two

THE KNOWLEDGE CONCERNING GOD BEING OUR LIFE

Scripture Reading: John 6:54-57; Col. 3:4

In this chapter we will consider life.

GOD BEING OUR LIFE

God's children do not have a thorough and accurate view concerning the divine life. Although many children of God love Him, fear Him, and are pious, not many know that God is their life. The fact that every believer has the life of God seems to be a doctrine, because few believers practically experience God as life every day. Many believers are proper and good, but few genuinely live in God and take Him as their life.

We must learn the difference between persons who are proper and good and persons who live in God and take Him as their life. Do not think that a well-behaved person lives in God or that a God-fearing person lives by God. To be well-behaved or God-fearing is different from living in and by God.

As believers, we should know the purpose of salvation and know the meaning of Christianity. There are many groups in Christianity, but the majority of them teach only a kind of religious piety. They neither see nor express the divine life. Strictly speaking, Christianity is not a religion. The Christian faith is not a matter of behavior but a matter of life. Christians are not followers of a religion. Christians have received Christ as their life because Christ entered into them when they believed in Him. However, most of God's children do not know this. The new believers among us must know this matter.

I knew that I was saved nearly thirty-five years ago. I will never forget the way I that was saved. Even though I had never heard that the Lord can meet man, on that day I had to admit that the Lord met me. I was a young person who loved the world, loved my future, and had likes and dislikes. However, the Lord met me and saved me. I was not saved out of a fear of going to hell or a desire to go to heaven. Rather, I was saved because I saw that without God, my life would have no meaning. Even if I gained the whole world, I would still be empty without God in my life.

One day I heard the gospel of how mankind is under bondage and slavery in the world, of how this world usurps man and keeps him from turning to God, and of how empty and vain life is when man puts God aside. The Lord opened my eyes, and before the message was finished, I said, "O God, if this is the case, I do not want the world any longer. I want only You." I did not know whether this was a prayer or a vow. I only knew that after I said this, my inner condition changed. When I left the meeting place, I felt light, as if I were flying in the air. On my way home I prayed, "I do not want the world anymore. I want only God."

This is the way that I was saved. At the time of my salvation, I did not confess my sins, nor did I know that I was a sinner. I only felt that I was a person following the world. I wanted the world, education, future fame, and a position; I wanted a good future. After I was saved, I discovered that I was corrupt and had numerous sins. Later I read in the Bible that the Lord bore all my sins on the cross (1 Pet. 2:24) and that my sins were forgiven (Col. 1:14).

I loved the Lord after I was saved. I enjoyed praying, and I enjoyed reading the Bible. As far as I was concerned, the Bible was a sweet book. Not only did I spend time reading it every day, but I also read it before going to bed every night. When I woke up in the morning, I would pick up the Bible and read a few lines before getting up. Furthermore, while getting dressed, I would meditate on what I read. This is the extent to which I loved the Bible.

I also enjoyed praying. I often had the urge to go to the mountain or to the seashore in order to pray. I dared not sing of the Lord Jesus' name, because as soon I sang, I would burst into tears. The sweetness and loveliness of the Lord became an indescribable power that caused temptations, sins, lustful things, and the world to drop off of me.

Nevertheless, even though I was so close to the Lord, I did not know that He was my life, nor did anyone tell me this. I often went to a group of people who were capable of expounding the Bible and giving the best messages. They gave five messages per week, and I never missed a message, even when there was two feet of snow outside. For seven and a half years I listened to about two thousand messages.

I thought the messages were enjoyable. The speakers had a thorough knowledge of the Bible and were able to connect the whole Bible from Genesis to Revelation. One of the persons there was called a living concordance because he was able to give the book and chapter of any verse that was quoted from the Bible. These believers were able to speak in detail concerning the signs, numbers, types, and prophecies in the Bible.

However, I never heard them say that the Lord Jesus came to be life to man. They said that those who believe in the Lord Jesus would receive everlasting life. But they never said that this everlasting life is the eternal life of God. I had heard the term *everlasting life* innumerable times, but I had no idea what it meant. No one told me that everlasting life is eternal life, which is God and also the Lord Jesus. The God who came into me is the Lord Jesus, and He is also eternal life; He came into me to be my life. No one told me this.

One day the Lord had mercy on me and showed me the way of life. Then I began to consider, "What is the purpose of expounding the signs, numbers, types, and prophecies in the Bible? These messages are not life, but people need life." As a result, I stopped going there to listen to the messages.

From that time onward, I had a great turn. The Bible in my hand changed completely. I was familiar with the Bible and could recite many portions accurately because I had spent seven years studying the Bible. When I realized that the Lord was life to me, the Bible became a new and living book to me. Whatever I read in it became a matter of life. Ever since that day God has led me to see life. In particular, for the past ten years I have not been able to give a message that is not concerning God being our life. If I did not speak of God being our life, the message was empty. God has not given me any other burden. God in the Son and through the Spirit has entered into me to be my life. The Triune God is in us to be our life.

God's unique thought is to be our life. If you ask me what God wants to do with us, I would answer, with full assurance, that He has no desire to do anything other than to be our life. Perhaps you think that God wants us to do many things, but these things are not central or important. The central thought of God is that He wants to enter into us to be our life.

MAN'S NATURAL, RELIGIOUS CONCEPTS

Man's thoughts concerning God are about how to worship, fear, and please Him. When a person enjoys the world and does evil things, he puts God aside and does not care about God. When he receives mercy and turns to God, he begins to think about God and care for God and immediately desires to worship God, do things for God in order to please Him, and do His will. Man cannot escape from such thoughts.

Even the messages that are preached among Christians are according to the concept of worshipping God and doing things to please Him. Preachers tell people how to worship God, how to obey His will, how to please Him, and how to do things for Him. These concepts and teachings are natural; they are man's natural, religious concepts and are not according to God's intention.

I once visited the second largest mosque in the world and saw many Moslems worshipping. Their worship involved prostrating their whole body. Although they displayed indescribable solemnity and devoutness, it was truly pitiful. They expended a substantial amount of energy in order to worship God, but they did not know that God does not care for that kind of worship.

What does God want? Religionists and Jewish rabbis might say that God wants people to worship Him. Muslim imams might say that people should wash themselves and bow down to God reverently five times a day. Catholic priests might say that it is best to attend mass every day. Even Christian pastors and preachers might say that we should learn to pray quietly and worship God. These are all religious answers. They are man's natural concept. They are not what God wants.

THE REVELATION OF GOD IN THE BIBLE

The Bible does not teach us to do something for God. In the beginning of the Bible there is a blueprint, and at the end of the Bible there is a building. If we compare the building with the blueprint, we will know what God wants to do in the universe and in man.

In the beginning of the Bible there is the tree of life, and at the end there is also the tree of life. In the beginning of the Bible the tree of life is outside of Adam (Gen. 2:8-9), but at the end, in the book of Revelation, the tree of life is inside the holy city, New Jerusalem (22:1-2). The New Jerusalem is a corporate man and includes the New Testament saints who are represented by the twelve apostles and the Old Testament saints who are represented by the twelve tribes of Israel (21:12, 14). In the New Jerusalem man will no longer be facing the tree of life; instead, the tree of life will be in man.

Although the tree of life was outside man in the beginning of Genesis, God's intention was for the tree of life to enter into man. The tree of life is a fruit tree, and the fruit was to be man's food. Hence, when God placed man before the tree of life, His intention was for man to eat of the tree of life. At the end of Revelation the tree of life has entered into man.

In the blueprint presented in Genesis 2 there is a flowing river producing gold, bdellium, and precious stones (vv. 10-12). At the consummation of the Bible, in Revelation, there is a river of water of life flowing throughout the city (22:1), and the city is constituted with gold, pearl, and precious stones (21:18-21). These two pictures are a reflection of one another.

This shows that God's intention is not for man to worship Him or serve Him outwardly, nor is it for man to do anything for Him. God is pleased to be man's life. He placed Himself before man as the tree of life so that man would take Him in.

Genesis 2 does not show that God was sitting on a glorious brightly shining throne surrounded by cherubim and angels and commanding Adam to worship Him. On the contrary, God was manifested before Adam in the form of a tree. He did not display His power or splendor, nor did He require Adam to do something. He only asked that Adam would receive Him as food.

John 1:4 says, "In Him was life." Later, the Lord said, "I am the true vine" (15:1). These verses show that the Lord is the tree of life mentioned in Genesis 2. He has no intention for man to worship Him, serve Him, or do anything for Him. His desire is for man to receive Him, not to receive something from man outwardly but for man to receive Him as food inwardly.

In the Gospel of Matthew a Canaanite woman cried out, "Have mercy on me, Lord, Son of David!" (15:22). She wanted the Lord to do something for her, but the Lord Jesus answered, "It is not good to take the children's bread and throw it to the little dogs" (v. 26). The Lord was bread given by God to His children, and hence, He should not be given to dogs. The Canaanite woman had wisdom from the Holy Spirit, and she said, "Yes, Lord, for even the little dogs eat of the crumbs which fall from their masters' table" (v. 27). She seemed to be saying, "Yes, Lord. You are the bread, yet today You are not on the table; You were thrown off the table to the ground. You have been debased by God's children in the land of Israel, and You are in the Gentile land. The land of Israel is the table, and the Gentile land is under the table. You are the bread given by God to the people of Israel, but they were naughty and improper and threw You, the bread, off the table. Hence, a little dog such as I can eat the crumbs which fell from the table." The Lord Jesus praised this woman and said, "O woman, great is your faith!" (v. 28). This shows that the Lord Jesus considered Himself to be the bread of life that came down from heaven (John 6:35, 51), and as such, He desired to enter into man. He wanted man to eat Him and receive Him so that He might be man's life.

TAKING THE LORD AS LIFE
AND LIVING HIM OUT

God's purpose is not to teach doctrine or to correct our behavior. His purpose is life. God knows that we cannot do His will or do anything for Him out of ourselves. However, if we receive Him as food daily, taking Him as our life, we will do His will. Even though we may not think of pleasing Him, everything we are will be pleasing to Him, and we will spontaneously worship and serve Him. All the situations in our living will have His flavor, and He will be expressed through us.

A brother once said that some people smell like cows because they drink much milk and eat much butter and beef. They eat the produce of cows every day, so eventually they smell like cows. We smell like what we eat. The things in the physical realm are symbols of things in the spiritual realm. The Lord Jesus said, "As the living Father has sent Me and I live because of the Father, so he who eats Me, he also shall live because of Me" (v. 57). A person who receives the Lord as food will live and grow by the Lord, and he will also "smell" of the Lord.

May the eyes of the young saints be opened to see that God does not want us to worship Him, to serve Him, or to do something for Him. He is still standing before us as the tree of life. He is in His Word and the Spirit, waiting for us to use our spirit to receive Him. We should take Him as life, and let Him live in us (Col. 3:4). This is a glorious matter. As long as we can lay hold of this matter, we will have many glorious experiences of expressing Him. This is the story of life.

CHAPTER THREE

THE STEPS OF GOD ENTERING INTO MAN
TO BE MAN'S LIFE

Scripture Reading: John 1:1; 4:24; 6:63; 14:6; 2 Cor. 3:17

A MYSTERY—FIVE YET ONE

John 1:1 says that "the Word was God." Here *Word* does not refer to a brief word but to a long speech. In New Testament Greek, both *logos* and *rhema* are translated as "word." *Logos* denotes a long speaking; it is the constant word. *Rhema* denotes a brief word; it is the instant word. The Word in John 1:1 is *logos*.

John 4:24 says, "God is Spirit, and those who worship Him must worship in spirit and truthfulness." The first part of 6:63 says, "It is the Spirit who gives life." Here the expression *gives life* has two meanings in the original Greek: to cause people to have life and to cause people to live. Hence, an expanded translation is, "It is the Spirit who causes people to have life and live." The second part of this verse says, "The words which I have spoken to you are spirit and are life." *Words* here is *rhema,* that is, short and instant words. In John 14:6 Jesus said, "I am the way and the reality and the life." Second Corinthians 3:17 says, "The Lord is the Spirit."

The verbs in the above verses are important. The Word *is* God, God *is* Spirit, the words that the Lord speaks to us *are* spirit, the words that the Lord speaks to us *are* life, the Lord *is* life, and the Lord *is* the Spirit. These are six instances of the verb *to be* concerning the following items: the Word, God, the Spirit, life, and the Lord. God, the Lord, and the Spirit refer to the Triune God. The three of the Triune God plus the Word and life are five items.

The verb *to be* in these portions can be likened to an equal sign that links all five items together, making the five items one. The Word is equal to God, God is equal to the Lord, the Lord is equal to the Spirit, and the Spirit is equal to life. It is amazing that five items are one item. These are five truly mysterious items, yet the five items are also one.

GOD ENTERING INTO MAN TO BE MAN'S LIFE

God desires to enter into man to be man's life. This is His purpose. Everything else that God does relates to this purpose. In other words, God's purpose depends upon God entering into man, being man's life, living in man, and living out of man. A seed is a good example. When the life in a seed is activated, the seed will sprout, and a stalk and leaves will grow. This plant will continue to grow until it blossoms and bears fruit, in which are more seeds. In this endless cycle, life is produced and duplicated. We can say that the purpose of a plant is to blossom and to bear fruit and seeds. However, everything in this cycle depends on life.

God's purpose, His intention, is to enter into man to be man's life so that He can live in man and then be lived out of man in every situation. We need a change in our concepts. We should not have the religious concept of worshipping God, serving or working for Him, doing things that He needs, pleasing Him, or being pious. Although these may be good, they are religious concepts and are not God's purpose. God's purpose is to enter into us in order to be our life and then to be lived out of us in all things.

THE STEPS OF GOD ENTERING INTO MAN

God enters into us to be our life in three steps.

God Dwelling in Eternity Past as the Father

The Bible says that God dwells in unapproachable light (1 Tim. 6:16). The Bible also says that God inhabits eternity (Isa. 57:15) and that His name is Eternal Father (9:6). Eternity transcends time and space. There is no way for man to contact the God who dwells in eternity. In His holiness, He is like a consuming fire (Heb. 12:29). Anyone who would attempt to approach Him would be consumed. Hence, it is impossible for man to contact the God who dwells in eternity, let alone to receive Him as life. This is the first step.

God Being Manifested among Men as the Son

We thank God that in addition to being the Father, He is also the Son. Thus, He is able to contact man. He is God, and He is the Lord; He is the Father, and He is the Son. As the Father, He is hidden, but as the Son, He is manifested. Every one of us is someone's son; hence, we have a father. We usually ask people if they have sons, but we never ask if they have a father. As long as a person exists, he must have a father. A man is the manifestation of his father. This is what the Bible means when it refers to the Father and the Son. The Father is the source of the Son, and the Son is the manifestation, the expression, of the Father. The eternal God who dwells in unapproachable light is the source; this is the Father. One day He was manifested; this is the Son. John 1:18 says, "No one has ever seen God; the only begotten Son, who is in the bosom of the Father, He has declared Him." When Philip asked the Lord to show them the Father, the Lord rebuked him, saying, "Have I been so long a time with you, and you have not known Me, Philip? He who has seen Me has seen the Father; how is it that you say, Show us the Father? Do you not believe that I am in the Father and the Father is in Me?" (14:8-10). These words show that the Father and the Son are one. We might say that the Son hidden is the Father and that the Father manifested is the Son. The Son is the manifestation of the Father, and the Father is the source of the Son. The two are one. Hence, in the second step, God came in His Son, the Lord Jesus, to be manifested among men.

God Entering into Man as the Spirit

In the second step God was merely among men. He was manifested among men, but He still had not accomplished His purpose, which is to enter into man as man's life. If God cannot enter into man, He will not become man's life. If God wants man to worship Him, to serve Him, to please Him, to obey His will, or to work for Him, it is sufficient for Him to stay outside of man. However, in order to be man's life, He must enter into man. He cannot be man's life unless He enters into man. Hence, as the eternal God who dwells in unapproachable light, He cannot be man's life. Neither was it sufficient for Him to be manifested among men, because He still could not be man's life. In order to achieve His purpose of becoming man's life, the Son had to be transfigured. The Father was manifested as the Son, and the Son was transfigured as the Spirit. God is embodied in the Son, and the Son is realized as the Spirit so that He can enter into us as life. This is the third step.

Chapter 14 of the Gospel of John is a turning point. The first thirteen chapters speak of the Father being manifested in the Son, that is, the Word becoming flesh and dwelling among men. However, He could only dwell among men; He could not enter into men. Then in chapter 14 the Lord said to His disciples, "If I go…I am coming again" (v. 3). His going was His coming. His going was His suffering death, and His coming was His resurrection. By His going and coming through death and resurrection, He was transfigured to be the Spirit. Through such a transfiguration He is now able to enter into us. His going was His coming (vv. 2-3). He came to us as the Comforter, who is in us and will be with us forever (vv. 16-20). Before chapter 14 the Gospel of John does not speak of the Lord being in His disciples and of their being in the Lord; rather, it speaks of the Word becoming flesh and dwelling among men. In chapter 14 the Lord began to speak of His entering into man. This turning point depends on His coming as the Spirit.

In the evening on the day of the Lord's resurrection, while the doors were shut where the disciples were for fear of the Jews, the Lord came and stood in the midst of them (20:19). No one knows how the Lord came in; this is something we do not understand. The Lord Jesus stood among the disciples and breathed into them and said, "Receive the Holy Spirit" (v. 22). The Bible does not tell us where the Lord went after He breathed into the disciples.

In chapter 13 the Lord washed the feet of the disciples. After washing their feet, He spoke to them at length for three chapters, chapters 14 through 16. After speaking with the disciples, He prayed, and His prayer is recorded in chapter 17. After praying, He took the disciples to the Garden of Gethsemane, where He was seized, and He was taken to the high priest and to Pilate to be judged; this is chapter 18. In chapter 19 He was nailed to the cross and put into a tomb. In chapter 20 He was resurrected, and He first ascended to the Father God. Then in the evening the Lord appeared to the disciples and breathed into them, saying, "Receive the Holy Spirit." The Bible does not tell us where He went after this. However, on the evening of the next Lord's Day He came again and said to Thomas, "Bring your finger here and see My hands, and bring your hand and put it into My side." Thomas answered and said to Him, "My Lord and my God!" Then Jesus said to him, "Because you have seen Me, you have believed. Blessed are those who have not seen and have believed" (vv. 27-29). Again the Bible does not tell us what happened next. Thus, we do not know where the Lord went. Then in chapter 21 the disciples went fishing for a whole night but caught nothing. Suddenly, the Lord Jesus appeared on the shore and invited them to breakfast. After breakfast the Lord asked Peter three times, "Do you love Me?" (vv. 15-17). Then He said, "Follow Me" (v. 19). Again we are not told where the Lord went after this incident.

It seems as though the Lord disappeared. Some people have said that the Lord ascended to heaven. However, chapter 21 does not record the ascension of the Lord Jesus. Where did the Lord go? He said, "In that day you will know that I am in My Father, and you in Me, and I in you" (14:20). The Lord entered into the disciples. He entered into them as the Holy Spirit. The Father was manifested among men in the Son, and the Son was transfigured as the Spirit to enter into man. When the Son was transfigured as the Spirit, He could enter into man. The Spirit enters into man to be man's life. God the Son can enter into man because He has been transfigured as the Spirit. God is Spirit.

Perhaps some do not understand this. They think that the Father, the Son, and the Spirit are three and wonder how can They be one. This is truly a mystery, but here is an illustration. When we take an ice cube out of the freezer, it will become water after a period of time. Although ice and water have different forms, they are actually one. Water is ice, and ice is water;

the two are one. If we keep the water out of the refrigerator for a whole day, it will evaporate, disappear. The water will become vapor. Vapor has a different form from water, but vapor is water, and water is vapor; the two are one. Hence, ice is changed into water, and water becomes vapor, which is in the air for man to breathe. When we breathe in vapor, we are breathing in water, which is also ice. The three are one. Although this illustration cannot fully describe the relationship between the Father, the Son, and the Spirit, it at least provides a general explanation.

Similarly, the Father was manifested as the Son, and the Son was transfigured as the Spirit. Revelation 5:6 speaks of the Spirit being sent forth into all the earth. Hence, the Spirit fills the universe; He is omnipresent, not being limited by time or space. The Spirit is present at any time and in any place. This Spirit is the Son, who is the embodiment of the Father. The Father is in the Son, the Son is in the Spirit, and the Spirit fills the universe. Hence, regardless of time or place, the Triune God will touch a person whose heart is turned to God, whose spirit is open, and whose inner being is aligned with God. The Father, the Son, and the Spirit will immediately touch his spirit and move in his spirit.

THE WAY TO HAVE GOD AS OUR LIFE

Touching the Spirit

Do we want God? Do we want to obtain Him and allow Him to enter into us? In the Old Testament God was intangible and could not be found. But today He is real; He is not vague. God is embodied in the Lord Jesus, the Lord Jesus has become the Spirit, and the Spirit has been sent forth into all the earth. The Spirit is everywhere; He is omnipresent and ever-penetrating. Today He is waiting for proper persons with a proper heart and a right spirit. Wherever there is a broken and contrite heart with a spirit that is turned to God, that is, a person whose heart and spirit believes and who confesses the Lord Jesus as his Savior, the Spirit of the Triune God will enter into this person. Thus, this person will obtain God. The Father is in the Son, the Son is in the Spirit, and the Spirit enters into man. Thus, this person has the Triune God in him as his life.

He has the Father, the Son, the Spirit, and eternal life; he has four items.

Contacting the Word

If there were only the Father, the Son, the Spirit, and life—without the Word—our obtaining God would be vague. However, the Lord is not only the Spirit but also the Word. The Gospel of John says that the Word is God, that God is Spirit, and that the Lord's words are spirit (1:1; 4:24; 6:63). If we consider these verses together, we can see that God is not only the Father, the Son, and the Spirit but also the Word. In order to enter into man to be man's life, God became a man, the Son, and was transfigured into the Spirit. However, we still need to touch or sense Him in a concrete way. Thus, He is also the Word. The Word is real. If I am asked where we can find God, I would say in the Word and the Spirit, for the Word and the Spirit are God. Regardless of where a person is, if he uses his heart and spirit to read God's Word, the Spirit will touch his inner being and bring the Triune God into him, because the Word conveys the Spirit. When this Word is manifested within man, it is *rhema,* the instant word, which is also the Spirit.

Initially, the Bible is the constant word, *logos.* When we read the constant word with our heart and our spirit, the ever-penetrating Spirit will touch our spirit and will shine on every word that we read so that He can manifest Himself within us. Then every word and every sentence will become living and operative. This is *rhema.* The living, instant word is spirit and life. Hence, when we receive these words, we receive the Spirit as well as life. At the same time, we also receive the Triune God. The Father, the Son, and the Spirit will enter into us through the Word to be our life. Hence, we will touch and receive life; that is, we will receive the Triune God. This experience of the Triune God as the Word and life in man is the most central and mysterious matter in the universe.

CHAPTER FOUR

GOD BEING THE ELEMENT OF LIFE

Scripture Reading: John 20:28; 10:18; Heb. 2:17-18

The purpose of the Triune God is to dwell in us to be our life. In order to enter into us, God has worked in three steps. God dwells in unapproachable light (1 Tim. 6:16). One day, as the Word, He was incarnated and manifested among man in order to be with man (John 1:1, 14). Then after thirty-three and a half years He died on the cross and was resurrected to become the Spirit (Rom. 1:3-4; 1 Cor. 15:45). He became the Spirit so that He can enter into those who believe into Him (John 20:21-22). This is how the Triune God enters into man as life. God the Father is the source, and man cannot approach or touch Him. This God is embodied in the Son and was manifested among man. Then He died and was resurrected to become the Spirit in order to enter into man. These are the three steps that God took to enter into us.

THE ELEMENTS OF GOD

The Triune God with all His elements has entered into us. We often neglect God's elements. When we consider God, we think of Him as being the Father, Son, and Spirit, but there are other elements within God. The elements of the Triune God, that is, what is in Him, are not so simple. There are at least seven elements.

The Element of Divinity

The first element of God is His divinity, His divine nature. When God enters into us to be our life, we receive the divine nature of God.

The Element of Humanity

God also has the element of humanity, the human nature. Before He became flesh, He was purely God; He had the divine nature. One day, however, He became a man; He put on humanity and was mingled with man. Thus, He possesses not only divinity but also humanity. Some saints have been saved for many years, but they do not realize that the Lord whom they worship and in whom they believe is not merely God but also man. I hope that we can see this fact. When God was incarnated, He put on humanity, and the human element was added to Him.

After the Lord Jesus was resurrected, Thomas said to Him, "My Lord and my God!" (20:28). At that time the Lord was not merely God; He was also a man. Before incarnation, in the Old Testament, God was only God; He did not have the human element. But in the New Testament God was incarnated; He became a man and was mingled with man. Furthermore, through His death and resurrection, He brought man into God. Hence, in John 20:28 He had not only divinity but also humanity. The human element was added to God.

The Element of Human Living

God possesses the element of human living. God became flesh and lived on the earth as a man for thirty-three and a half years. This is something that He did not have before His incarnation. For thirty-three and a half years the incarnated God lived on the earth. On one hand, this man was the holy God, but on the other hand, He lived as a genuine man.

The Gospel of John says that the Lord Jesus is God, and it also shows how He lived as a man. In chapter 3 He received a Jewish ruler, who was a proper man, at night. In chapter 4 He was in a different situation, in which He contacted an infamous woman. He met her during the day in an open area. The matter of time and place speaks of how a person conducts himself. What kind of impression would we have if the Lord had received the infamous woman in the same way that He received the Jewish ruler, that is, at night? How would that influence us?

The Lord Jesus also knew that it would not be appropriate to discuss the woman's history while His disciples were present. He knew that she would be greatly embarrassed, so He waited alone at the well to talk to her when she came. Furthermore, the Lord did not speak severely when He touched the details of her background. He simply followed her words. He said, "You have well said, I do not have a husband, for you have had five husbands, and the one you now have is not your husband; this you have said truly" (vv. 17-18). How tactful the Lord was, yet His words hit the mark. This situation shows the condition of His being a proper man. He is Lord, and He is God. As God, He does not need to care for such details, but He did. This is an aspect of His human living.

In chapter 7 the Lord's flesh brothers came to Him and said, "Depart from here and go into Judea;...for no one does anything in secret and himself seeks to be known openly. If You do these things, manifest Yourself to the world" (vv. 3-4). His brothers thought that it was the time for Him to go up to Jerusalem for the feast, but He replied, "My time has not yet come, but your time is always ready" (v. 6). This shows another aspect of His human living. From the aspect of being God, He transcends time and is not limited by time. However, at this point, He was a man and was living the human life; hence, He was willing to be subject to various restrictions. This shows that the Lord has not only the human element but also the element of human living.

According to Hebrews 2:17-18, the element of human living includes the suffering of temptations and afflictions: "Hence He should have been made like His brothers in all things...For being tempted in that which He Himself has suffered, He is able to help those who are being tempted." He also suffered temptations, in which He had contact with the devil and experienced how the devil tempts man. In other words, He fought the battle with the devil, and He did it as a man. Before God became flesh, He was God, but He did not have the experience of being a man. Hence, He was without the element of suffering through temptations. Because He lived as a man for thirty-three and a half years, He has not only the element of divinity but also the element of human living, including the experiences of suffering, being tempted, and overcoming the devil.

The Element of Death

God possesses another element, which is death. He has experienced death. Although death could not hold Him or keep Him, the element of death was added to Him when He passed through death. Some saints might react to this statement. They might say, "How can the element of death be in the ever-living God? This kind of speaking is dangerous." Please do not misunderstand the meaning of these words. There is good death and bad death. We know that without the Lord's death, there would not be a way for us to be saved. The Lord's death is a great salvation, a great door, to us. Satan had trapped us in Adam's sin, but the Lord's death opened a door for us and released us from sin. Hence, His death is a good death. Moreover, His good death puts to death and terminates not only our old creation but also Satan, the world, and all things other than God. We praise the Lord that the element of death is in God.

The Element of Resurrection

The fifth element is resurrection. The Lord Jesus died and also resurrected. He manifested life in death. Hence, He is not only life, but even more He is resurrection. In John 18 and 19 the Lord was seized, judged, and nailed to the cross. These situations of death manifested that He is life. It seemed as though Satan put Him to death, but actually He laid down His life (10:18). Most people do not die willingly; they are dragged into it, and they have to die. Only the Lord Jesus was not dragged into death; rather, He walked into death. When He was about to be seized, He said, "I am," and the people who came to seize Him drew back and fell to the ground (18:5-6). Nevertheless, He still went with them. This shows that He walked into death. He did not seem to feel the threatening attack of death.

After being seized, He was taken to be judged. However, He was not the person being judged; rather, those who judged Him were being judged by Him. By standing before them, it was manifested that He was the Judge. The judgment of death manifested His death-overcoming life. This shows that He is life in death. Then He was crucified. Death by crucifixion is the most cruel punishment. The pain one experiences in crucifixion is beyond description. However, by enduring such pain, the Lord manifested that He is life and that He could not be subdued by the pain of death. While He was being crucified, He still cared for His mother and said to her, "Behold, your son," and then He said to John, "Behold, your mother" (19:26-27). From these situations we can see that although death tried its best to destroy Him, it could not subdue Him. His life in such death situations can be likened to a flame of fire in the midst of ice cubes; not only are the ice cubes unable to quench the fire, but the ice cubes are melted by the fire. This is similar to life being manifested in death.

The Lord's life is so strong that He was not afraid of death but was able to resurrect from death. Resurrection is stronger than life. Resurrection is life breaking forth from death. Nothing can hold Him, because He is resurrection. When He resurrected, He broke through Hades, death, the tomb, and every bondage. Hence, the element of resurrection was added to Him.

The Element of Man Entering into God

When the Lord resurrected from death, He brought man into glory; that is, He brought man into God. He is the glorious and exalted God. When He became a man, that is, when the Word became flesh, He brought His glory into lowly man. He had the appearance of a Nazarene, a carpenter, and a man from a poor family. His visage was marred, and He had no attracting form nor majesty. People thought that He was nearing the age of fifty when He was only in His thirties (Isa. 52:14; 53:2; John 8:57). He was a lowly man. If we were to describe Jesus the Nazarene, we would call Him lowly.

However, glory was hidden in His lowliness. When the Lord became flesh and brought glory into lowly humanity, He did not lose His glory. Do not think that He was merely a Nazarene and the son of a carpenter without majesty. In His inner being there was glory. One day He was on the mountain and was transfigured; His inner being came forth, and the disciples saw Him enveloped in glory (Matt. 17:2). However, this glory was revealed only for a short while; then it was hidden again. This was God entering into man and glory being brought into lowliness.

Then the Lord Jesus was resurrected. In His resurrection He brought man into God; that is, He brought lowliness into glory. His incarnation brought glory into lowliness, and His death and resurrection brought lowliness into glory. He brought man into God. When Stephen was martyred, he saw the heavens opened and the Son of Man standing there (Acts 7:56). At that time a man, the resurrected Lord Jesus, was in the heavens. He is in the heavens with His humanity. He brought man into God and lowliness into glory. Today there is a man in the glory. Everything is glorious. Hence, the resurrected Lord has the element of man entering into God.

The Element of Ascension

God also has the element of ascension. The Lord ascended and entered into heaven with His humanity. We should not consider heaven to be merely a place. Of course, heaven is a place. However, when the Bible speaks of the Lord Jesus' ascension into heaven, it does not refer merely to heaven as a place but to the nature of heaven. When the Lord Jesus ascended, He entered into not only the place of heaven but also the heavenly nature.

Our old man is out of the earth and is earthy (1 Cor. 15:47). Earth is not merely a place but also a nature. Hence, to say that man is earthy means that earth is the nature of man because he is made of earth. Similarly, to say that the Lord Jesus ascended to heaven refers more to the nature of heaven than to the place of heaven. The Lord Jesus is not only in heaven as a place but also in the nature, condition, state, characteristic, and atmosphere of heaven. Hence, He brought man not only into God but also into heaven. Now He is enabling man not only to have the glory of God but also to have the nature of heaven.

SEVEN ELEMENTS

In summary, God possesses seven elements: the element of divinity, the element of humanity, the element of human living, the element of death, the element of resurrection, the element of man entering into God, and the element of ascension. If a person in the Old Testament had received God into him, only one element, the element of divinity, would have entered into him. But God is no longer in the Old Testament. He became flesh, lived as a man, died, resurrected, brought man into God, and ascended into heaven. Hence, these seven elements are within Him. As a result, when we receive Him into our spirit, His seven elements enter into us.

I beg you to use your spirit to absorb this word and to use your mind to memorize it. Our ability to remember this word will affect our life practices in the future. We must be clear that the Triune God is now the Spirit with many rich elements. He has the elements of divinity, humanity, human living, death, resurrection, man entering into God, and ascension. As long as a person is saved, the Triune God is his life; hence, he should immediately begin to experience these seven elements. Even a new believer who has been saved for only two or three months can still experience these seven elements.

EXPERIENCING THESE SEVEN ELEMENTS

When we received the Triune God into us, we received the divine nature; the Holy Spirit brought God into us. Hence, we are human beings, and God is within us.

We also have the Lord's humanity. Some may say that they are already human beings. This is true; however, we should consider whether we were more proper as human beings before we were saved or after we were saved. Many believers were not very proper before their salvation; they did not have much weightiness. After their salvation, however, they began to have some weightiness and to conduct themselves like proper human beings. If they will pursue the Lord more and be filled more with the Holy Spirit, they will become more proper and weighty as human beings. This is the experience of God working within man. A person who has God within him is much weightier than a person without God. In other words, the God who enters into this person brings with Him the element of humanity so that this person can live the life of a proper man.

We have also received the element of human living. After a

person is saved, his conduct changes. Prior to his salvation, he may have been careless in his speech when he interacted with others. After he is saved, there is no need for him to be taught; he spontaneously becomes sober and clear. His relationship with others, regardless of their gender or age, is no longer careless; rather, it is sober. He can discern whether a matter concerns females or males, whether it is related to the elderly or to the young ones, and whether it should be dealt with by only believers or also unbelievers. He can also discern how to speak with others, based on their situation. When we allow God to live in us, we will take care of our living and our walk; we will be conscious of our measure. The life that has entered into us has an element that causes us to know how to live as proper human beings.

Some saints have the erroneous concept that it is sufficient to have God and be filled with the Holy Spirit. They think that they do not need to take care of their living. Such Christians neglect the aspect of their human living; they do not take care of the way they dress, the way they live, or the way they deal with others. This is not proper. The thought that a person who is spiritual does not have to care for a proper living is a wrong concept. The more spiritual we are, the more we will live in the Lord, and the more He will cause us to live as proper human beings.

Miss M. E. Barber was a sister from the West who served the Lord in China for many years. She was very spiritual and knew the Lord. For a period of time, there was a group of young brothers and sisters who often went to her to be taught. Some of these young saints neglected being proper in their human living because they pursued being spiritual. Sometimes Miss Barber would call one of the sisters into her room, bring out a mirror, and ask, "Please look in the mirror, and see how you combed your hair. Have you combed your hair in the last three days?" Miss Barber would speak frankly, saying, "Sister, it is right that you are pursuing spirituality, but you are not a spirit or an angel. You are still a human being; hence, you need to learn how to be a proper human being. You should care for your appearance, just as you care for spiritual matters." Miss Barber was right. The more a person grows in the

Lord, the more human he will become; he will bear a strong aroma of a proper humanity.

When the Triune God enters into us, He brings with Him the element of death. As long as we pursue the Lord, fellowship with Him, and enjoy His presence, the power of death will operate within us to cause us to die to the world, to sin, to the flesh, and to fleshly reactions. The closer we draw to the Lord, the more we will be filled with Him. The more we allow Him to operate in us, the more we will sense the killing power of death in relation to all things. The power of death is in the Lord's life.

We will also experience being in resurrection; nothing will be able to suppress, imprison, oppress, or restrict us. A brother's wife might have a physical weakness; there might be various problems or difficult situations pressing upon him. From the human point of view, he might not have the strength to bear his environment. However, he can experience a power that enables him to gradually stand in the midst of his problems and difficulties. This is the element of resurrection.

Not only so, as believers, we sense that we are in glory. This is not pride, nor is it a boast, but it is a spontaneous sense. In our daily living we should be persons in glory, persons in God.

We might argue with a taxi driver over a small matter such as the taxi fare, but there is no glory in this situation. Rather, it shows that we are still earthy and do not see how glorious we are. At times I also have wanted to argue with the taxi driver, but when I was about to open my mouth, a voice within me said, "Do not forget that you are a man in glory." Immediately, I would drop my argument. Sometimes I have even given the driver a little more money.

Whether or not we are right, we can never feel good when we argue with others. We will always feel that we are earthy and short of glory. In contrast, if instead of arguing we concede to others, we will sense that we are in glory. We will also sense that we have entered deeper into God.

When I have contacted people with a high social status, I am respectful toward them, but I do not feel lower than them. We should not be proud, but we have entered into God; the lowly have entered into glory. I believe that we all have had such experiences.

Furthermore, as believers, we sense that although we live on earth, we do not belong to this earth; we belong to heaven. We are persons not only in God but also in heaven. Earthly things will not touch us because we transcend the earth; we are in ascension.

These points are not doctrine; they are experiences of God for us. The more we touch life and are filled with the Spirit, the more we will experience these elements. The element of divinity and the element of humanity will cause us to be weighty. The element of human living will enable us to be proper persons. The element of death kills the things within us that are not God. There is also the element of resurrection that gives us the power to break though everything that suppresses us. We also have the element of glory that gives us the sense that we are men in glory, men in God. Not only so, we also sense that we are heavenly. Even though we live on earth, we belong to heaven; we are persons living in the heavenly realm of ascension.

Such experiences can be our experience when God is life to us. God has passed through incarnation, human living, death, and resurrection. He has also brought us into Himself as well as into the heavenly realm. All that He has passed through has become His elements. All these elements are in the Spirit, and the Spirit has entered into us. Hence, all these elements have become ours. The more we live by God as our life, the more these elements will increase within us and become stronger and more apparent.

CHAPTER FIVE

TAKING GOD AS LIFE AND LIVING BY HIM

Scripture Reading: Gen. 3:22-24; John 1:1, 4, 14; 6:57; 14:10; 12:24; 19:34; Heb. 4:16; 10:19-20

GOD DESIRING MAN TO RECEIVE HIM AS LIFE

Most people have the concept that they should worship and serve God and do something for Him. This, however, is not what God requires of man. At the beginning of the Bible, God presented Himself as food to man so that man could receive Him (Gen. 2:8-9). He wanted man to receive Him as food so that He could enter into man to be man's life. The first two chapters of Genesis show that among all the creatures created by God, man is the highest creature and possesses the highest life. Man has God's image and likeness to express God and to represent Him with authority, that is, to rule over everything created by God (1:26). However, man did not have God's life; God was not in man. God wanted man to receive Him as life. Therefore, after He created man, God placed man before the tree of life.

The tree of life indicates that God wants to be man's life. God placed Himself before man as the tree of life, indicating that He wanted man to receive Him as food. God wants to enter into man to be man's nourishment and even become man's constitution, just as the food we eat becomes our nourishment and our constitution. In this way God is mingled with us as one, and we can live by Him and because of Him. He wants to be our life, and He wants us to express Him. This is the desire of God's heart.

If we can receive God, live by Him, and let Him live in us, we will have many wonderful experiences. God has no intention for us to do something for Him. What He asks of us is that we allow Him to enter into us to be our life and do everything through us. He wants us to do everything by Him as our life. In other words, what we do is secondary. The primary matter is that we take Him in as life. This is His primary thought.

THE FALL BEING TO NOT LIVE BY GOD

Before man received God as his life, the devil seduced man and caused him to receive the tree of the knowledge of good and evil instead of the tree of life. Thus, man fell away from God's goal. The tree of life points to God, and the tree of the knowledge of good and evil points to Satan. The result of eating the tree of the knowledge of good and evil is death (2:17), and Satan is the source of death. The tree of the knowledge of good and evil denotes Satan, who has the might of death (Heb. 2:14). On one side of man was the tree of life, which denotes the God of life, and on the other side of man was the tree of the knowledge of good and evil, which denotes Satan with the might of death. The tree of the knowledge of good and evil indicates that death is expressed as good, evil, and knowledge. The result of contacting God is life, but the result of contacting Satan is death. God expresses Himself as life, but Satan expresses himself as good, evil, and knowledge. Satan uses good, evil, and knowledge to seduce man away from God and the divine life.

The real meaning of man's fall is that instead of choosing God as his life, man chose good, evil, and knowledge. Whenever a person chooses good, evil, or knowledge instead of God as life, that person is in the fall. Adam fell when he turned to the tree of the knowledge of good and evil. This same principle applies to us today. When we attempt to do things apart from God's life, we have departed from the tree of life and have received the tree of the knowledge of good and evil. The result of such a choice is death. This is a serious matter.

Many of God's children know the difference between good and evil but not the difference between life and good. When we see a brother who is humble, polite, and loves others, we say that he is a good brother. When we see a brother who rebukes and mistreats others, we say that he is a bad brother. It is easy to differentiate between good and bad, or good and evil. However, it is not so easy for us to determine whether the humility of a humble brother is of life or whether it is of himself. Life is the expression of God, but good is merely something worked out. If a brother is able to love others and is humble and meek without needing to let God be his life, his conduct is good but not life. His living is not the result of God living out from within him, and God has no place in his living. When we let God be our life, live by Him, and let Him live out of us, we are in life. When we deny ourselves and cooperate with God by allowing Him to operate in us, He will bring us into loving others, and He will become our humility and our meekness. On the surface, there is no difference in our love, humility, and meekness, but in actuality, our love, humility, and meekness are God. Instead of merely being our outward goodness, they are an expression of our inner life.

Regrettably, many of God's children do not know the difference between good and life. They know to condemn evil, but they do not know to condemn good. Both those who commit sins and do evil and those who are good and do good deeds are living according to the tree of the knowledge of good and evil; they are not touching life. In other words, they remain in the fall of man. We do not need to commit sins in order to be in the fall. We are in the fall when we do not live in God as life.

Suppose a brother habitually gambles, goes dancing, and even lives in dissipation; we would all say that he is in the fall. Suppose another brother bears some responsibility in the church meetings, likes to preach the gospel, and enthusiastically participates in various services; we would say that he is not in the fall. However, his activities do not necessarily indicate that he is not in the fall. We must ask whether he serves by God or by himself. Is this his pious and religious living, or is it the living out of God as life? If he does not live by the life of God, his piety is in the fall. This is not a fall from good to evil or from serving God to committing sins but a fall from living by the divine life to living apart from the divine life, from being in God to being apart from God.

We need to see that the fall of man is a matter of man not letting God be his life. Just as man is capable of doing evil things without the life of God, he is also capable of doing good things without the life of God. Regardless of whether man does good or evil, as long as he is apart from the life of God, not taking God as life or living by God, he is fallen.

THE LORD JESUS BEING THE FIRST PERSON TO TAKE GOD AS LIFE

Adam fell when he took of the tree of the knowledge of good and evil, thus allowing the element of Satan to enter into him. As a result of Adam's fall, God closed the way to the tree of life, using the cherubim and the flaming sword to guard it (Gen. 3:22-24). This means that the way to God was closed. Cherubim signify God's glory (Ezek. 9:3; 10:4; Heb. 9:5), the flame signifies God's holiness (Deut. 4:24; 9:3; Heb. 12:29), and the sword signifies God's righteousness (Lam. 3:42-43; Rom. 2:5). God used the cherubim, the flame, and the sword to close the way to the tree of life. This means that His glory, holiness, and righteousness do not permit fallen man, with the element of Satan, to contact Him. Thereafter, no fallen human being on earth could contact God or receive Him as life.

One day God was manifested in the flesh (1 Tim. 3:16); there was a man on earth who took God as life (John 1:1, 4, 14). When the Lord Jesus was on the earth, He let God be His life. He was a genuine man with the human life and nature. Apart from the fact that He was without sin, He was exactly the same as us. He came to the earth to live as a genuine man, but He took God as life and lived the human life by God's life.

The Lord said, "The living Father has sent Me and I live because of the Father" (6:57). The phrase *because of* indicates that although the Lord Jesus was a man, He did not live by Himself; He lived by God. He took God as the factor of His living. Therefore, He could say, "The words that I say to you I do not speak from Myself, but the Father who abides in Me does His works" (14:10). Apparently, the Lord was speaking, but actually, it was God who was working. This was a man who did not live by His own life but took God as His life. It was not until the Lord Jesus was born that God gained a man on earth. On one hand, the Lord Jesus was a genuine man with His own mind, emotion, and will; He had choices and preferences. On the other hand, He completely denied Himself, put His own life aside, and let God live in Him; He let God be His preferences and choices.

The Lord Jesus was not without thoughts, but He denied His thoughts and let God think in Him. It was not that He did not know how to choose, but He chose God's choices. He denied everything of Himself and took God as His life. He was a human being, but He lived by God. This is the greatest event in the universe. It is immeasurably greater than God's creation of the heavens, the earth, and all things on the earth. Although the Lord Jesus was only an insignificant man from Nazareth, having no beauty, splendor, or glory, He was mingled with God, and God was His life. This is the greatest and the most mysterious thing in the universe!

God wants to obtain the very same thing in us. We should not think that God wants us to worship Him, serve Him, or do something for Him. God desires that we learn to receive Him and to take Him as our life by denying ourselves, just as the Lord Jesus did.

RECEIVING GOD AS LIFE THROUGH THE CROSS

In order to gain His desire, God sent the Lord Jesus to die on the cross. There are two significant aspects of the Lord's death on the cross: the redemptive aspect in which His blood was shed to deal with man's sins and the life-releasing aspect in which the divine life was released from within Him for man to receive. As descendants of Adam, we have an evil nature within us, and we are sinful. Hence, God's righteousness, holiness, and glory do not permit us to go before God or to contact Him. For this reason, the Lord Jesus needed to accomplish redemption. On the cross He bore our sins, and He also received the righteous judgment of God, thereby satisfying the requirements of God's righteousness, holiness, and glory. As a result, He removed the barrier between God and fallen man, and He opened a new and living way to God (Matt. 27:51; Heb. 10:19-20).

On the cross the Lord Jesus also released the divine life. In John 12:24 He said, "Unless the grain of wheat falls into the ground and dies, it abides alone; but if it dies, it bears much fruit." This verse refers to the life-releasing aspect of His death.

A marvelous thing happened when the Lord died on the cross. According to Roman law, in order for those being crucified to expire quickly, their legs were broken. For this reason, the soldiers broke the legs of the two robbers who were crucified together with the Lord. However, when they came to the Lord, they saw that He had already expired, so they did not break His legs (19:32-33). This fulfilled the words in the Scriptures: "No bone of His shall be broken" (v. 36; Psa. 34:20). The first time a bone is mentioned in the Scriptures is in Genesis 2:21-23 when God took a rib out of Adam for the producing of Eve. This symbolizes the producing of the church with Christ's resurrection life. Hence, the bone is a figure of Christ's unbreakable resurrection life. The fact that not one of the Lord's bones was broken means that His resurrection life was neither damaged nor subdued by death; rather, it was manifested and released through death.

John 19:34 says that a soldier pierced the Lord's side with a spear, and immediately there came out blood and water. Blood is for redemption, and water is for imparting life. This water was typified by the water that flowed out of the cleft rock (Exo. 17:6; 1 Cor. 10:4). Hence, blood and water indicate what the Lord accomplished through His death on the cross. The blood indicates that He accomplished redemption to deal with man's sins, and the water indicates that He released His life for His believers.

Now we can receive the divine life to become His many grains. Just as the Lord had God as His life and lived because of God, so also we can have the Lord's life and live because of Him. His blood dealt with our sins and thus satisfied the requirements of God's righteousness, holiness, and glory. Therefore, we can contact God with boldness. We can also receive Him as living water so that we can live by Him.

What does it mean to believe in the Lord Jesus? The Lord Jesus has done so much for us. First, when He lived on the earth, He set up a pattern of a genuine man who let God live in Him and also lived by God's life. After living such a pattern, He is now producing many people who are like Him. He was the grain of wheat that fell into the ground in order to produce many grains. On the one hand, He had to shed His blood in order to bear man's sins; on the other hand, He had to release His life in order to impart it into man. Now man can draw near to God with boldness through the Lord's blood, and God can enter into man to be man's life. This fulfills His desire to fill man and flow out of man as living water. This is the issue of believing in the Lord Jesus and receiving Him as life.

God's intention in saving us is to enter into us as life. Therefore, after we are saved, we should take heed to letting Him be our life and to letting Him live in us, fill us, and be expressed through us. Our primary responsibility is neither to serve God, to work for Him, to obey His will, nor to worship Him. These are not the primary matters that God wants us to pursue.

TAKING GOD AS LIFE AND LIVING BY HIM

We can take God as life and live by Him by eating, drinking, and enjoying Him. In John 6:57 the Lord said, "As the living Father has sent Me and I live because of the Father, so he who eats Me, he also shall live because of Me." When we eat and enjoy the Lord, He will carry us in our living and in our service, and we will spontaneously do His will.

God became the Spirit so that He can enter into our spirit. He knows that this matter is too vague for us to comprehend; hence, He has given us the Bible. In other words, in addition to entering into us as the Holy Spirit, He is also present in His Word so that we may contact Him. As Christians, we have the Bible without and the Spirit within; we have the Bible in our hand and the Spirit in our spirit. Now we can contact God as the Spirit and in the Word.

When we use our spirit to contact the Bible, God's Spirit will touch our spirit. The more we contact the Word, the more the Spirit will move in our spirit. The move of the Spirit within us is the divine life in us. We should simply follow His move and cooperate with His anointing. If He wants us to weep, we should weep, and if He wants us to rejoice, we should rejoice. When He wants us to preach the gospel, we should preach the gospel. When He does not want us to speak, we should stop speaking. If He does not want us to go to a certain place, we should not go. We should cooperate with and obey His move. This is what it means to take God as life and live by Him.

I hope that all the saints will practice taking God as life and living by Him. We should set aside some time daily to contact God's Word and allow the Holy Spirit to touch our inner being through the Word. We cannot contact the Word merely by reading the Bible in an ordinary way or by studying the Bible with our mind. We should use our spirit to contact the Word. We need to spend time before the Lord and contact God's Word with our spirit. Then the Holy Spirit will touch our spirit.

The Word is the expression of God, and the Spirit is God entering into us. The Word enters into us as the Spirit. The Word is the Spirit, and both the Word and the Spirit are God. The Word is outside of us, and the Spirit is inside of us. When God's speaking enters into us and when we touch the Spirit, God becomes our life. If we learn this secret, we will experience and enjoy Him as life every time we contact the Word.

This is not doctrine; it is a practical way to take God as our life. Hence, we should practice contacting the Word and the Spirit with our spirit.

CONSECRATING TO TAKE GOD AS LIFE

Let us be more subjective. In order to take God as life by contacting His Word and letting His Spirit touch our spirit, we must take another step: we must consecrate ourselves. Consecration does not mean that we should do something for God. Rather, consecration means that we should cooperate with God to let Him live in us and be our life. I must proclaim to all God's children, "God has no intention for us to do anything for Him!" He wants us only to cooperate with Him to let Him live in us. Nothing is more pleasing to God than our cooperating with Him by letting Him live in us.

It is one thing for a believer to have the divine life, but it is another thing for him to let God live in him. These are two different things. About twenty years ago I lived in Chefoo in northern China. In those days not many houses had electricity; many homes still used kerosene lamps. After electricity was installed in my home, I would often light a kerosene lamp out of habit. One night I returned home and immediately went to look for matches. My family asked me, "What do you want the matches for?" I said, "To light up the kerosene lamps." They laughed and said, "We have electric lamps now." I realized that this is similar to our experience: God is in us, but we are not used to applying or enjoying Him. Rather, we are accustomed to living by our own life. Hence, after we are saved, we forget that God has come into us to be our practical living. Even after hearing many messages concerning God as life, we still live by ourselves, just as I had the habit of lighting a kerosene lamp instead of switching on the electric lamps.

May God open our eyes to see that there are two lives within us. We have our human life and God's life. We have been habitually living by our human life. Hence, we know that we should not do what is wrong, bad, or evil. However, we spontaneously try to do what is good and right because we are used to doing such things. For example, a brother may have the concept that he should not use bad words. However, he does not practice contacting God to know whether or not he should speak, even if he wants to use good words. He does not know what it is to deny the self and forsake the natural life. He does not know the difference between speaking by himself and speaking by the life of God.

We are not asking whether a certain thing is good or bad. We are asking whether we are doing things by our human life or by the divine life, that is, whether we are living or whether God is living. There is a big difference between our doing something alone and God doing it in us. Most of the saints still desire only to forsake evil and do good. They are content with doing good things. This is the concept of an ethical or a religious person, but it is not taking God as life. This is a matter of ethics and religion, not of life. The matter of life requires that we take a step further and ask whether we are doing a good thing by our human life or by God. Are we the ones living, or is God living in us? Are we doing something independent of God, or are we doing it together with Him? There is a big difference here.

When we learn to discern between such matters, we will know what it is to take God as life practically and what it is to express the divine life. In order to live by God and let Him live in us, we need to have a thorough and definite consecration. We should say, "Lord, I see a fact: You want to be my life, and You want to live in me. This requires that I cooperate with You. Hence, I consecrate myself completely to You. Although I have the human life and live as a man, I am willing to learn to forsake myself and take You as my life. I am willing to cooperate with You and let You live in me. I am willing to give myself to You as a vessel for You to fill me, to move in me, and to be expressed through me. Lord, I reject my will, my mind, and my views. I want to take Your will as my will, Your mind as my mind, and Your views as my views. I do not want to take myself as the standard; I want to take You as the standard and as my life."

How many saints have consecrated themselves in such a way? I first consecrated myself because I did not want the world, but I wanted to serve God. Hence, I prayed, "Lord, from this day onward I give myself to You. I want to be used by You and to serve You." On another occasion I felt that I needed to be filled with the Holy Spirit. Hence, I had a thorough consecration in which I gave myself completely to the Lord. However, when I saw that God wants to live in me and that He wants me to take Him as life, my consecration was much more thorough. After seeing God's desire, I said, "O God, I give myself to You, not to work for You or to be filled by You but to let You be my life. You are the glorious, bountiful, and holy One, and I want You to live in me. Therefore, I give myself to You as a living vessel. I would no longer live by my own life. I give myself to live by You and to take You as life."

Such a consecration is deeper than a consecration with the purpose of being used by God or of being filled by the Holy Spirit. Many saints still have not had this kind of consecration. I encourage these saints to have a definite consecration. They should find a quiet place and from the depths of their being give themselves to God in a specific way. They should say, "Lord, I have seen that You want to live in me as my life and that You need my cooperation in this matter. For this reason, I am consecrating myself to You as a living vessel. I have a strong desire to move with You when You move and to stop with You when You stop." This is not a matter of being guided or led by Him but of our letting Him live in us as our life so that we can live by Him.

In order for the messages that we have heard in the past to become our experience, we need the work of the Holy Spirit. However, we also need to cooperate by consecrating ourselves. Without such a consecration, it will be difficult for the Spirit to work in us. The Spirit is willing to operate in us, but if we are passive and not absolute, lacking the standing of consecration, He will not be able to do anything. If we are willing to consecrate ourselves, it will be easy for the Spirit to move in us.

Suppose I would like to shake hands with a brother. If he does not cooperate by lifting up his hand, we cannot shake hands. If he understands my intention and reaches out for my hand, we can shake hands. This is the way that the Spirit works in us. He needs our cooperation. The Spirit earnestly desires to work in every one of us, but He cannot do anything if we do not give Him the opportunity by cooperating with Him. The Spirit can be compared to air or the wind, which is able to enter through an open door or window. He can also be compared to water, which is able to flow into any crack. The worst situation is for a believer to be like a room without any openings; the wind cannot blow in, air cannot seep in, and water cannot flow in. Some saints are like a room with iron walls toward God. They are saved, but they are not concerned about God being their life. They have heard messages and understand that He wants to be their life, but they remain the same because they have not exercised their spirit to receive what they have heard.

This message is vain if a believer remains indifferent and noncommittal, being unwilling to have an absolute, definite, and thorough consecration. I hope that every brother and sister will have a thorough consecration. We should not give ourselves once to the Lord; we should renew our consecration daily, just as the Israelites offered the burnt offering every day. We should say, "I am a normal human being, but I do not live according to my human life. Lord, I let You be my life and live in me."

If we will consecrate ourselves in such a way, the next time we come to the Bible, it will be living, bright, and fresh, and we will touch God with our spirit. Not only so, we will experience Him moving in us and anointing us; we will sense that God is living. If we maintain our consecration, we will have unceasing fellowship with God. This unceasing fellowship is what John 15 describes as abiding in the Lord. In such a fellowship the Lord abides in us, and we abide in Him, just as branches abide in the vine. The branches that abide in the vine take the vine as their life, and the sap of the vine becomes the element of the branches. As a result, the branches grow leaves, blossom, and bear fruit.

The fruit borne on the branches is the expression of the life of the vine. The fruit is not the result of conduct, work, or self-cultivation; rather, fruit is the issue of the growth of life, an expression of life, and a flowing out of life. This is a picture of what God wants to gain in us. He does not want us to work for Him or to merely carry out His will. He wants us to let His life be lived out of us, to be expressed through us. On His side, He has done all that He needs to do. He became flesh, died, resurrected, ascended to the heavens, and became the Spirit. Furthermore, He has mingled Himself with man and mingled man with Himself. He has done everything.

He is now waiting for us to cooperate with Him. He needs us to have a definite response of letting Him be our life. If we are willing to respond by consecrating ourselves thoroughly, He will spread and gain ground in us, item by item, until He occupies our entire being. He will motivate us to live according to Him. When we live according to Him, we are letting Him live in us; that is, we are taking Him as our life practically. This is what God desires.

CHAPTER SIX

LIVING BY THE INNER OPERATION
OF THE RESURRECTION LIFE

Scripture Reading: Eph. 3:7, 20; Phil. 3:10; Col. 1:28-29

The basic matter in God's work is His intention to enter into man to be man's life. Christianity, however, has lost this basic matter. Without knowing God as life, Christianity is only a religion. When Christianity lost the truth of God as life, it transmuted into a religion.

God does not intend for us to be adherents of a religion. He desires that we receive Christ into us as life so that we may become people who receive Christ as life and let Christ live out of us. Hence, we do not proclaim a religion; we proclaim Christ. According to the Bible, Christ is not only the Redeemer; He is also life. Christ is our Redeemer so that He may be our life. His being our Redeemer is but a procedure; His purpose is to be our life. He accomplished redemption for us, as fallen sinners, so that we would be His vessels and that He would be our life and live in us. This is God's intention. When God achieves this, His heart's desire will be fulfilled.

GOD AS LIFE BEING A GREAT MYSTERY

God's children have never regarded the matter of God as life in a serious way. This is a problem. For more than ten years after I was saved, I did not understand that God is my life. Many good things have distracted God's children from this matter. The Triune God is great and infinite, but He desires to dwell in our human spirit. He also wants all that He is to be in us as our life. The divine life is beyond our comprehension; it is a mysterious matter.

A seed is small and insignificant. When it is cut open, it

looks so ordinary that it is hard to believe that there could be anything mysterious in it. However, when the seed is planted in the soil, all that is contained in the seed will gradually grow forth. A small seed can eventually grow into a tall tree. A seed can at least grow to be a sizable plant with green leaves, flowers, and even abundant fruit. Without these various outward expressions, no one would believe that so much is contained in a small seed.

Similarly, it is difficult to gain a thorough knowledge of the mysterious divine life. We can sense that we are sinful; hence, we understand that the Lord Jesus bore our sins on the cross. We have repented, believed in the Lord, and are now saved; hence, we have peace and joy. We are clear concerning these things. However, we do not have much feeling concerning the Triune God entering into our spirit to be our life. This seems to be a light and ordinary matter.

All the riches of God, His fullness, dwell in Christ the Son bodily, and Christ the Lord is now the Spirit (Col. 2:9; 2 Cor. 3:17). This Spirit entered into us when we believed in the Lord Jesus. We did not receive a part of the Spirit. Rather, He entered into us as the complete Triune God. Hence, just as the Triune God is rich in Himself, He is rich in us. We do not have only a portion of His riches. If we could see the riches of this treasure in us, we would experience joy unspeakable.

When I was in Tientsin in 1936, the Lord pointed out to me that He is the same in me as He is in Himself; there is no difference. The God in me is the complete God; He is not lacking anything. When I saw this fact, I was beside myself. I wanted to tell everyone, "Come and see! Here is a man who has God in him. The complete God dwells in me!"

We need to see the treasure that we received when we were saved. This treasure is God with all His riches. This treasure is God with His experiences of incarnation, human living, crucifixion, death, resurrection, ascension, becoming the life-giving Spirit, entering into man, and bringing man into God. The fullness of the Godhead with all these experiences entered into us as the Holy Spirit to be our life. When we see this, we will be overjoyed.

One evening in the summer of 1932, before the first church

in northern China was raised up, a Christian visited me, and we talked about many matters. As we walked and talked, we came to the seashore and talked about baptism. I quoted several verses to show him what the Bible says concerning baptism. When it became late and I suggested that we go home, he held my hand and said, "You cannot go home now. You must baptize me in the sea." I said, "I am neither a pastor nor a preacher. I am just a young man in my twenties. How can I baptize you?" He held on to me and said, "You are all words with no action. You just told me the kind of people who are qualified to be baptized and the kind of people who can baptize others. Please consider whether you are qualified. I will let you go home, if you say that you are not qualified. Otherwise, you must baptize me tonight." Hence, we knelt down there at the beach and prayed. After we prayed, we went into the water, and I baptized him. When he came out of the water, his joy was beyond description. The next day when he saw me, he said that he was so happy he could not sleep.

If every believer saw what he received at the time of his salvation, he would be beside himself with joy. We received the rich and glorious Triune God—the Father, the Son, and the Spirit. Very few believers experience this kind of joy when they are saved. Usually believers know that their sins have been forgiven and that God loves them. They might say, "I was a prodigal son, but He found me and brought me home. I deserved death; I was going to hell, but He rescued me." We have heard such testimonies from many brothers and sisters after their salvation. However, they did not see the treasure that they have received when they were saved. What they saw was merely a shell, the covering of the treasure.

Precious jewelry is sold in a beautifully decorated box. A child would rather have the beautiful box than the treasure in the box, because he is confused and does not know what is precious. Many believers are just as confused as a child with a box. They do not have much feeling related to the treasure within them. They sense only that their sins have been forgiven and that they will not perish in the future. Little do they realize that this is merely the shell of their salvation. In God's salvation He Himself is the center. God, with all that He is, is salvation. When we receive His salvation, we receive God. Salvation is precious, but God is even more precious. As believers, we all must see this.

BEING A CHRISTIAN
BY THE POWER OF RESURRECTION

The emphasis of God's salvation is that He has given Himself to us. Hence, our being a Christian depends on our having a normal relationship with the indwelling God. The Bible shows that God dwells in us in order to be our life. Not only does He lead us in every matter, but He wants to be the power of our living. This power is the power of His resurrection. The Lord Jesus went into death, and although death tried its best, it could not hold Him. On the third day the Lord broke through death and Hades, and He ascended to the heavens, transcending everything. This was accomplished by the resurrection power. Resurrection power enabled a Nazarene to break forth out of death and to ascend to the heavens. Such a resurrection power has entered into us to become our life.

Several places in the New Testament use a particular word in relation to the power that raised Christ from the dead. In the original Greek the word *operation* or *operate* is often used (Eph. 1:19-20; 3:7, 20; Col. 1:29). The resurrection power that operates in us is not harsh; it is gentle and refined but nonetheless very powerful.

Many Christians do not realize that there is such an operation within them. Hence, they are Christians outwardly but not Christians according to this inner operation. For example, a newly saved brother desires to learn how to live before the Lord. When he draws near to the Lord, this inner operation will give him the sense that he should spend more time to fellowship with the Lord and to have a thorough dealing. If he continues to fellowship with the Lord instead of being distracted, the operation within him will intensify. As a result, he will have a thorough dealing with the Lord. He will also enter deeper into God and let God enter deeper into him. While he is learning to fellowship with the Lord, a few brothers might encourage him to preach the gospel. If this young brother is active by disposition and also eloquent, he will feel happy while preaching the gospel. However, when he turns to outward things, he may become an outward Christian. Initially, he was experiencing the operation of the resurrection power within him. However, he may be distracted and begin to focus mainly on outward activities. It is good to preach the gospel, but some people cannot turn back to the inner operation after they are distracted and become involved merely with outward activities. Thus, this brother can become an outward, zealous Christian who is busy with many outward activities in the service but does not understand the inner operation of life.

Many years ago I met a gospel preacher in Shantung province. Before his salvation, he was an emaciated opium addict. One day he was genuinely saved, and he threw away his opium pipe. Then he put on weight and became plump and healthy. When he preached the gospel, he carried two pictures with him: one picture of himself looking emaciated and another picture of himself looking plump and healthy. He said that he was an advertisement for the gospel. However, this brother had merely dropped his bad habit and changed from being skinny to being plump; he knew nothing concerning God being life to man. He was energetic in preaching the gospel, but when he lost his temper, he was terrifying. At the time I met him, I was giving messages, and he came every day to hear the messages. The strange thing was that before and after the meeting he was interested to speak with me about gospel preaching, but he was not interested in hearing the messages that I was giving concerning life. From his speaking I was clear that he was a zealous Christian who lived in outward activities but knew nothing of the life within him.

We should preach the gospel, but the gospel should be preached by the operation of resurrection life. The apostle Paul was a minister of the gospel, but his gift of preaching the gospel was not out of his natural ability or natural eloquence. His preaching the gospel was the issue of the resurrection power that operated within him. This gift was produced in him by the resurrection life.

I know a brother who, after being dynamically saved, completely forsook all evil activities. He no longer desired the world, was clear concerning God's calling, and consecrated himself.

He liked to pray and to read the Bible. When he drew near to the Lord, he experienced the Lord's operation within him. He told me of how the Lord operated in him. Although his mother had not spoken with him for many years, the Lord asked him to apologize to his mother. This was truly the operation of life within him. He received much light in reading the Bible, was desperate to understand the Bible, and desired to be a preacher. He often asked me, "Where can I go to learn the Bible? Where can I go to learn to serve the Lord?" I would reply, "Brother, your living is your Bible school. If you live fully in the church life, you will learn to serve the Lord." However, he was quick by disposition and was not willing to learn to know God's life in his daily living, to allow the divine life to grow in him, or to know the Bible according to life. Neither was he patient enough to coordinate with others in the church in order to learn to serve the Lord according to the measure of life. While he was in this situation, a pastor who also loved the Lord encouraged him to study theology. As a result, he went to a seminary to study theology.

After four years he graduated from the seminary and came to see me. He said, "I learned Bible knowledge in the seminary and received much instruction concerning how to preach the gospel. However, I cannot touch God anymore. What is the reason?" I asked him how long he had been in this situation, and he said, "From the day I enrolled in the seminary, I was very busy with seminarian studies. As a result, my fellowship with God was interrupted. Ever since I began to study theology, the '-ology' replaced God in me."

Many Christians have the same problem. God has been in us from the day that we were saved. He is the God of resurrection, He is full of riches, and He is the God of great power. As such, He lives in us and is operating unceasingly within us. The most troublesome matter to Him is that we do not remain with His inner operation; we do not care about His operation in us. We often become outward Christians; we run around asking for advice and wanting to engage in various activities. As a result, not many people are inward Christians, and there are too many outward Christians.

A person who learns Chinese boxing must develop outward

skills as well as internal strength. Boxing with outward skills consists of many gimmicks and actions that appear exciting but are not of much value. Boxing with internal strength does not seem to have many actions, but it has much power. There are two kinds of Christians, those with "outward skills" and those with "inner strength." However, very few Christians have inner strength. Regrettably, Christians either indulge in sins and love the world, or they zealously preach the gospel, study theology, and are involved in Christian activities. Most pay attention to good behavior and working for the Lord. Such Christians have outward skills, not inner strength. God desires for us to be Christians with inner strength—Christians who afford His life, the resurrection power, the opportunity to grow in them.

Every plant grows slowly from the life within. A plant cannot be forced to grow fast. According to a Chinese proverb, any effort to make a plant grow faster would only pull up the seedling. There was a man who wanted to help his wheat grow faster, so he pulled on the plants. He did not know that his pulling on the wheat caused the plants to die. Often our efforts to help others is in the principle of pulling up a plant. We see that a brother is growing slowly, so we pull him up a little. However, we have not helped him grow faster, for after a short period of time he will wither and die. Hence, outward help is futile. If we desire a seedling to grow well, we should not attempt to pull it; rather, we need to loosen the soil and add compost so that nutrients and water can reach the plant and cause it to grow. Loosening the soil and adding compost and water will supply the plant, but pulling on the plant will cause it to die. Often instead of watering, adding nutrients, or loosening the soil, the saints pull when they visit people. As a result, people are "pulled out."

Furthermore, the leaves, flowers, and fruits of a plant are not added outwardly; they grow from within. Similarly, various Christian activities should be the result of growth from within; they should not be something added outwardly. The things that are added outwardly will not last long. They will wither and die after a short period of time.

These illustrations show that being a Christian is altogether an inward matter; it is not outward. Some people like to kneel down and pray for twenty minutes. Although it is good to kneel down to pray, such outward kneeling does not matter. What matters is whether we take care of the operating of God's resurrection power. Being a Christian does not depend on outward conduct, work, activities, or accomplishments but on taking care of God's operation within us. The apostle Paul said that God "is able to do superabundantly above all that we ask or think, according to the power which operates in us" (Eph. 3:20). Everything that God accomplishes for us is based on this operation.

Many saints wrongly apply Ephesians 3:20 to outward things and matters. A brother once testified, "I asked God for a bungalow. I prayed for half a year, and God gave me a two-story house. What God accomplished is above all that I asked or thought." Ephesians 3:20 does not refer to such things. According to this verse, what God accomplishes for us is altogether related to the inner life, to the operation of His power in us. Suppose a brother is giving me a difficult time, and I pray only for patience in order to not lose my temper. However, if I allow the resurrection power to operate in me, I will not only be patient and not lose my temper, but I will also love him in a sweet way. In this situation the power that operates in me has accomplished above all that I asked or thought. I hoped that the life within me would lead me to overcome, but I did not expect that this life would lead me to more than overcome. This life achieves above all that we can ask or think. This is the meaning of Ephesians 3:20.

Paul said that he labored to present every man full-grown in Christ and that his laboring was according to God's operation which operated in him in power (Col. 1:28-29). We must see that God's desire to be life in us and to live out of us is altogether an inner matter; it is not outward. This desire is accomplished by life growing within us, not by adding something outward to us. The resurrection power in us is constantly operating; hence, we should cooperate with this operation and live by it. In this way the divine life will grow in us, and we will live out this life practically.

CHAPTER SEVEN

THE FUNCTION OF GOD AS LIFE

Scripture Reading: John 14:16-17; 16:12-15; Rom. 8:2, 9; 1 John 2:27

John 16:13 and 14 say, "When He, the Spirit of reality, comes, He will guide you into all the reality; for He will not speak from Himself, but what He hears He will speak; and He will declare to you the things that are coming. He will glorify Me, for He will receive of Mine and will declare it to you." Verse 15 says, "All that the Father has is Mine; for this reason I have said that He receives of Mine and will declare it to you." There are references to four persons in verse 15. The first reference is to the Father, the second reference is to the Lord, the third reference is to the Spirit, and the fourth reference is to the believers. *All that the Father has* refers to the Father. *Is Mine* refers to the Lord. *He receives of Mine* refers to the Spirit, who receives from the Lord. *Will declare it to you* refers to the believers, who receive the Spirit's declaration. These words are very simple, but they speak of the crucial matter of the Triune God coming into the believers. The process of the Triune God coming into the believers begins with the Father and all that He has. All that the Father is and has, all His fullness, is in the Lord and is the Lord's (Col. 1:19). The Spirit receives the fullness of the Father from the Lord. The fullness of the Father is embodied in the Son and declared by the Spirit to the believers. The Spirit declares the fullness of the Father that is in the Son to the believers, making known to the believers all that He has received from the Son. This is the process of the Triune God coming into the believers.

The Triune God is the Spirit and the Word (John 4:24; 1:1). After the Lord Jesus died and resurrected, He became the life-giving Spirit (1 Cor. 15:45). The Spirit is omnipresent; He is everywhere. Hence, man can contact Him at any time and in any place. The Word is concrete. The Bible is a book that is in our hands, and the words of the Bible are often spoken to us. Hence, we can read the Bible with our eyes and hear its words with our ears. Whether we read or hear the words of the Bible, we should not contact them merely with our eyes or our ears; we should use our spirit so that the Word can enter into us as the Spirit. Hence, the Word is the Spirit, and the Spirit is conveyed in the Word. The Spirit and the Word are one. When the Spirit or the Word enters into us, they become life in us (John 6:63).

No person can say that he cannot touch God, because God has come forth. In order to come forth, He first became flesh (1:14), and then He became the life-giving Spirit (1 Cor. 15:45). His becoming flesh was His coming forth out of heaven, and His becoming the Spirit is for His entering into redeemed humanity. God the Spirit is omnipresent. Hence, no matter where a person is, as long as he is willing to use his spirit to contact God, he will touch God. The place where we can touch God is our human spirit. Hence, we must see the two spirits—the Spirit of God and the human spirit. God is Spirit. He became flesh, passed through death and resurrection, and became the life-giving Spirit. Not only so, God created man with a human spirit so that man would be a vessel to receive Him. Our created human spirit is the organ for us to receive God the Spirit.

GOD CREATING THE HUMAN SPIRIT
FOR MAN TO RECEIVE HIM

God created us with many organs so that we might receive the many things that are outside of us. For example, God wanted us to receive food and water, so He created us with a stomach. If we did not have a stomach, we would not be able to receive food and water. God wanted us to receive sound, so He created us with ears. Without ears, you would not be able to receive what I am saying. Similarly, in order for us to receive God, He created us with a human spirit. God is Spirit, and only the human spirit can touch, contact, and receive the Spirit. God created us with a human spirit so that we could receive Him.

The Function of the Human Spirit

We know what our eyes and our ears are, and although our stomach is not visible, we still know what it is. However, we might not know what our spirit is or where it is located. Many people have been saved for years, but they do not know that they have a human spirit. Some might know about their spirit doctrinally but not know how to experience their spirit. In the beginning God created man with a spirit. This spirit is not for us to receive food or sound; it is for us to receive God. If a person does not contact God or have any dealings with Him, his spirit is "unemployed"; that is, it has no function. This is the condition of many believers who do not use their spirit. They use their eyes, ears, lips, and brain, but they do not use their spirit; their spirit has been "laid off." The more we use an organ, the stronger it becomes, but an organ that we do not use will gradually wither. If a person covered his eyes so that he could not see any light, his eyes would lose their function after several years. Similarly, many believers cannot manifest their function, because they do not use their spirit.

When we heard the gospel, the Spirit came to touch our spirit. He first opened our mind to understand the truth of the gospel, and then He touched our heart. Our heart is closely related to our spirit; therefore, when the Holy Spirit touched our heart, He also touched our spirit. When we believed, our spirit was enlivened before God. As a result, genuine repentance and confession came from our spirit. The first time we repented and confessed before God, that repentance and confession came from the deepest part of our being. Hence, our spirit is the deepest part of our being.

Sometimes we have ample reasons to do something, because we have considered it with our mind. However, even though our mind agrees, we can have a feeling within that bothers us, that questions what we are doing. This shows that our intellect is one thing, but our spirit is another thing. We all have had this experience. Sometimes our spirit condemns us, saying that we are not proper. Although we may be able to defend ourselves with many reasons, in the deepest part of our being there is a sense or a feeling that we are not right. As we justify our actions, the sense within does not match. Thus, we discover that there are two persons in us. There is a person, our self, that likes to reason, and there is another person related to our human spirit.

The Chinese associate this second person with the conscience. Some people like to declare that they always speak according to their conscience. If they are asked how much money they spent on a certain item, they may say that they spent thirty dollars, but in their deepest part they know that this is false. If they respond to this sense, they will correct their speaking, saying, "I must speak according to my conscience. I actually spent only twenty dollars." The conscience is a part of the human spirit (Rom. 8:16; 9:1). The function of the conscience is the best proof that man has a spirit. The human spirit is the deepest part of man and is his most upright part. Most of the time our conscience does not stand on our side by excusing us; rather, it stands against us by accusing us (2:15).

Sometimes a person would argue with me and give many reasons to justify himself. Instead of arguing, I say to him, "Dear friend, you do not need me to say anything to you. Your deepest part has spoken to you on my behalf. You are arguing with me outwardly, but your inner being has already refuted you. I do not need to say anything. Moreover, the less I say, the clearer the speaking is in you."

Such examples show that there is a spirit in man. This spirit is the organ with which we receive God. If our heart is open to God, whenever our spirit moves, the Spirit will touch our spirit.

THE FUNCTION OF GOD AS LIFE
BEING TO SHINE IN US

The Triune God enters into us in order to be our life. The first function of His being life in us is to shine in us, to enlighten us (John 1:4). When we use our spirit to contact the Spirit, He shines in us. His shining causes us to feel that we are wrong or that we are defiled in different matters. Such feelings are the result of the Spirit's shining in us. These feelings, given to us by the Spirit as life, manifest the function of light. Hence, the manifestation of our touching the Spirit as life is that our inner being is bright, keen, and full of feeling. We might feel that we are wrong before our parents, that we are wrong in our attitude, or that we did not speak in a proper way. We will also sense that we have a motive in our love to God, that we have a preference in our work, and that our heart is not pure but is a mixture. Such is the issue of our touching the Spirit as life.

We can also say that such feelings are the result of the Spirit's shining. However, we must not forget that the shining of the Spirit is the manifestation of His being life in us. The more life we have, the more feelings we will have. In contrast, a lack of feeling indicates a lack of life. Our physical life is an example. When our physical body is healthy, our senses are keen and full of feeling. If someone touches us lightly, we will feel it. However, a dead person has no feeling because he does not have life.

A person who does not believe in the Lord has no feeling of shame when he sins or does evil or corrupt things, because there is no life in him. When he receives the gospel, the Spirit touches his heart and enlivens his spirit. Then he confesses his sins one by one according to his spirit, according to his conscience. This shows that his spirit is living. When his spirit moves, the Spirit is also moving in him as his life. The first function is to shine, to enlighten. The operation of the Spirit enlightens man and gives him many feelings.

Sometimes we do not draw near to the Lord for several days, nor do we exercise our spirit. Although the Spirit is in us, our spirit does not fellowship with Him, and as a result, we do not have much light or feeling. In such a condition we will not feel that something is wrong when we criticize or despise a brother, and we will defend ourselves when we mistreat others. Such situations indicate that we are short of taking the Spirit as our life. But when we exercise our spirit and confess our desolation, failure, and backsliding, the Spirit will operate in us, and our inner being will become bright. Then we will have a feeling before words of criticism leave our mouth, and we will be bothered within when we mistreat a brother, because the Spirit is operating in us as our life. When the Spirit operates, we are enlivened by His shining, and our inner being becomes bright.

TAKING GOD AS OUR LIFE
IN OUR LIVING AND OUR WORK

In Romans 8:2 the Spirit of God in us is called the Spirit of life. The Spirit is in us to be our life, not to do something. The purpose of His moving in us is not merely for us to do things but for Him to live out of us. Hence, those who know God as life do not pay attention to outward things; they focus on the Spirit living in them. When they give a message, their feeling is not that they are working but that the Spirit is moving, living, and being their life, which is manifested in their speaking. They do not feel that loving others is an outward activity. They love others because the Spirit is their life. They let the Spirit live in them and enable them to love others. From the human viewpoint, their loving others is a good behavior, but they know that the Lord is living in them and that they will feel bothered if they do not love others. Even their labor is the living out of Christ as life in them. For this reason, Brother Nee said, "Genuine work is the overflow of life." This can be compared to a fruit tree. We might say that the tree is bearing much fruit, but the tree would say that bearing fruit is the issue of its growing and the expression of its inner life.

The Triune God is in us to be our life; He does not have any other purpose. When we take Him as our life, the first thing He does is to shine, thereby showing us the things that are not right in us. The second thing He does is to supply us in everything that we do. He is our living and our work. He not only moves us and empowers us, but He also lives in us to gain our cooperation, thereby living out of us. He is expressed in our conduct, our living, and our work. Outwardly, we have good conduct, but our conduct and our work are the issue of taking the Spirit as life.

Our being enlightened when we read the Bible is not merely a shining but the Spirit living in us. If we do not allow the Spirit to live in us in the morning, we will not receive light when we read the Bible at noon. Sometimes God has mercy on us, and light shines into us as soon as we open the Bible.

However, that is not the normal situation. In a normal situation we should live in the Spirit and let the Spirit live in us all day. Then our reading of the Bible will be the result of the Spirit living in us and being our life. Furthermore, the shining function of the Spirit will be spontaneously manifested, and it will enable us to know the Bible.

We must see that the Lord is in us to be our life. If we let Him live in us freely, we will have many experiences of His growing and being expressed in us. These experiences include His shining, His supplying, and His leading. He supplies us with what we need. This is the secret of our joy, growth, overcoming, and spirituality.

CHAPTER EIGHT

HOW TO MAINTAIN FELLOWSHIP WITH GOD

Scripture Reading: 1 John 1:5-9; 2:27-28; 3:20-21, 24; 1 Tim. 1:5, 19; 2 Tim. 1:3

In the experience of God as life, there are several matters that are necessary in order for us to maintain our fellowship with God.

THE CLEANSING OF THE BLOOD

The first necessary item is the cleansing of the blood. First John 1:5 says, "God is light and in Him is no darkness at all." If we commune with God, fellowship with Him, and live in Him in a deeper way, we will be in the light, not in darkness. Light is for manifesting; the stronger the light becomes, the stronger its manifesting power becomes. At night we cannot see what is in a dark room. If we want to see what is in the room, we must turn on the light. During the day, when there is sufficient light, we can see everything in the room. However, if there is insufficient light, we will not be able to see any dust that is in the air. If the sun shines directly into the room, everything in the room will be manifested. Hence, light is for manifesting.

God as light has the same kind of manifesting power in us. The more we fellowship with Him and live in Him, the more His shining power will increase and intensify, and the various defilements in our being will be exposed. For this reason, 1 John 1 says that if we fellowship with God, we will be in the light, and we will see our sins (vv. 6-9). Before we receive the shining, we do not feel that we have any sins. But once we live in God, who is light, we will immediately be in the light, and all our mistakes, sins, defilements, and uncleannesses will spontaneously be exposed by the light. Some people may not feel that they have made many mistakes, but as soon as they enter into God's light, they will discover that they were wrong in many matters. Not only so, if they spend time in the light, their thoughts, intentions, desires, attitudes, and disposition will not remain hidden but will be examined under the shining of the light.

I once took my children to a science museum. The guide had a glass of what appeared to be clean water without any dirt. He took a drop of the water, put it on a glass slide, placed the slide under a microscope, and used a strong light to project an image of the slide on the wall. We were shocked because we saw many bacteria moving in the water.

Hence, whether or not a thing can be seen depends on the intensity of the shining it receives. The fact that many things cannot be seen does not mean that they do not exist; rather, it means that there is not enough light. If there is sufficient light, all things will be manifested. This applies not only to things in the physical world but also to spiritual things. We should not think that by not sinning or doing anything evil, we are good persons, and there is nothing wrong with our speech or conduct. If we enter into the light, many hidden things will be exposed. The light will manifest our living, conduct, speech, intentions, thoughts, motives, and attitudes. The closer we draw to God and the more we live in Him, the more our sins will be exposed by the light.

If we do not contact God, we will not know our true condition. When we take God as life and have deeper fellowship with Him, we are filled with light that exposes our sins. When our sins are exposed, our conscience immediately condemns us before God. This is when we need the cleansing of the blood. The first thing we need after we receive the shining of light is the cleansing of the blood. This is the fellowship of life in 1 John 1. God is light; hence, when we live in Him, we are exposed and our sins are manifested. At this time, we need the blood of His Son, the Lord Jesus, to cleanse us (v. 7).

No one knows the preciousness of the blood better than a person who lives by God's life. The more we fellowship with God, the more we will know the preciousness of the blood. As humans, we are born in the flesh, we grow up in sin, and we live in the world. Outwardly we are defiled, and inwardly we are corrupt. After we are saved, we still have the nature of the old creation, and we still live in the defiled world; hence, it is impossible for us not to be contaminated by sin. Only when we are away from God and without light can we say that we do not have sin. Those who say this are deceived and in darkness, because they are full of sin but without the feeling of sin (v. 8). Some saints like to criticize others and the church; they always find fault in others, but they never find any fault in themselves. Such a condition proves that they are in darkness.

One night while I was in my house, I noticed that the neighboring house was full of light. When I turned off the light in my room, I was in complete darkness and could not see myself, but I could see my neighbor very clearly. Whenever we do not sense that we are wrong but see others' faults clearly and criticize them, we are in darkness.

In contrast, if our house is flooded with light, but our neighbor's house is in darkness, we will not be able to see his condition; instead, we will see only our condition. Similarly, when we live in God, our entire being will be in the light, and we will see our sins. Before the rapture, we cannot reach a condition of being shined on by God yet having no consciousness of sin. Even if we do not commit any obvious sins, there will still be something in us that is incompatible with God. He is our life, and we are His vessel. Nevertheless, we are inadequate in our coordination and in our cooperating with Him. Hence, when we come into His light, our conscience will condemn us concerning many things. At this time, we will sense the need for the precious blood and apply its effectiveness. Thus, we realize that a person lives in God not only by His life but also through the blood. The blood enables us to maintain our fellowship with God.

THE ANOINTING

Another necessary item is the anointing. Concerning the anointing, 1 John 2 says that every believer has the anointing (vv. 20-27). The anointing does not refer to an ointment but to the action of applying the ointment. The anointing is the moving of the Spirit within us. The indwelling Triune God is always moving in us, and His moving is the anointing.

Verse 27 says, "The anointing which you have received from Him abides in you,…and even as it has taught you, abide in Him." We should abide in the Lord according to the anointing. We should speak when the anointing wants us to speak, keep quiet when the anointing wants us to be quiet, and move when the anointing wants us to move. This is the way to abide in the Lord and have constant fellowship with Him. If we do not obey the anointing, our fellowship with the Lord will be cut off. In our experience this means that we will not be in Him. Whether or not we abide in the Lord depends on whether we obey the anointing.

For the cleansing of a leper in the Old Testament, the priest would put blood on the lobe of the leper's right ear, on the thumb of his right hand, and on the big toe of his right foot. Then the priest would put oil on the lobe of the leper's right ear, on the thumb of his right hand, and on the big toe of his right foot (Lev. 14:14-18, 25-29). Wherever the blood was put is where the ointment was applied. The ointment could be applied only to the places that were covered with blood. The anointing ointment is God Himself. God is holy, and He is light. He cannot tolerate darkness, nor can He co-exist with wickedness. Hence, before He can anoint man with Himself, man must be cleansed by the blood.

First John speaks of the same sequence. There is first the cleansing of the blood and then the anointing. The apostle John wrote his Gospel and then his three Epistles. The Gospel of John says that God was incarnated to enter into us in order to be our life and that when we believe in Him, we receive His life. The Epistles of John, especially 1 John, say that since we have the life of God, we must live by this life and abide in this life in order to fellowship with God. In order to maintain this fellowship, two things are indispensable: the blood and the anointing. On the negative side, we need the blood, and on the positive side, we need the anointing. The blood cleanses us from the improper things within us, and the anointing anoints us with God. Whenever the Spirit as the ointment operates and moves within us, He anoints us with God.

The Spirit can be likened to a painter painting a table. Initially, the table does not have any paint on its surface. Then the painter applies paint to the table. The more he paints, the more the element of the paint is added to the table. Eventually, the table is filled with the element of the paint. This is the way that God anoints us. Each time that we allow Him to move in us, He anoints us with more of His element.

The anointing can be applied only to where the blood of Christ has been applied (Lev. 14:28). If we have not been covered with the blood, we cannot receive the anointing, and without the anointing, we cannot have fellowship with God. Hence, there must be the application of the blood and the application of the anointing ointment. The combination of these two makes it possible for us to maintain our fellowship.

When we were saved, we received the blood and then the anointing. The moment we repented, confessed our sins, and received the Lord Jesus as our Savior, the blood that He shed on the cross was applied to us, and the Spirit, who is the ointment, anointed us immediately. Thus, the Spirit began to abide in us. After our salvation we still need to fellowship with God and to abide in Him (1 John 2:28). As we abide in Him, we will see that we are defiled and sinful. This is when we need the blood to cleanse us. Once the blood is applied to us, the anointing ointment will follow. When the anointing is applied, the element of God will increase in us, and God as light will shine brighter in us. The brighter God's light shines, the more our sins are manifested, and as a result, we see that we need more of the cleansing of the blood. The cleansing of the blood ushers in a further application of the anointing, which in turn adds God's element into us. This is an endless cycle. The more times that this cycle is repeated, the more our naturalness will be washed away and the more we will be anointed with God's element. The more that this cycle is repeated, the more we will receive the shining of the divine light, and the cleansing blood will wash us of improper things. At the same time, the anointing ointment will add the divine element into our being. Eventually, everything in us that does not match God will be dealt with by the light and the blood, and we will be saturated with the element of God through the anointing. This is the genuine growth of life in the fellowship of life. Genuine growth in life is through the divine light, the blood, and the anointing.

A CONSCIENCE WITHOUT OFFENSE

The third necessary item is a conscience without offense. First John 3:20 says, "If our heart blames us, it is because God is greater than our heart and knows all things." God is greater than our heart; hence, when our heart blames us, God will blame us, and we will not have boldness toward Him (v. 21). Our heart blaming us is our conscience functioning within us. When our conscience operates, it blames us and causes our heart to lose its peace. The offense in our conscience comes from our sins. If we do not have light, our sins will not be manifested. Hence, an offense in our conscience is the issue of not receiving the shining of light.

When the divine light shines on any sin that we have committed, our conscience has an offense. We must deal with our conscience immediately; otherwise, the cleansing of the blood will cease. When the cleansing of the blood stops, the anointing also stops. This is terrible, because when the anointing stops, our fellowship with God also stops, and we will sense that we are not abiding in God but are outside of Him. Furthermore, instead of living by His life, we will live by our pitiful self. This is the greatest suffering of a Christian, and it is a miserable condition. In order to take God as life and live in Him, we must not neglect dealing with our conscience.

If we desire to learn to live in God, we must know the cleansing of the blood, the anointing ointment, and our conscience, which represents God's speaking in us. The condemnation in our conscience is God's demand in us as well as His speaking to us. The Spirit dwells in our spirit, and the main part of our spirit is our conscience. Hence, the function of our conscience is one of the functions of our spirit. When the Spirit anoints us, He adds the divine element into us. He also strengthens the shining of the divine light in our being, which causes our spirit to be bright. When our spirit is bright, our conscience manifests its function by condemning us and causing us to sense an offense. This is when we must deal with our conscience.

Hence, if we want to live in God and take Him as life, we

must deal with our conscience thoroughly. Otherwise, our fellowship with God will be broken. Some people may be saved, but they are careless Christians; they do not have much fellowship with the Lord. We cannot say that such a person has no feeling in his conscience; even though he is careless, he still has some feeling in his conscience. If he would be willing to deal with the feelings in his conscience, his fellowship with God would immediately be restored.

If we fellowship with God and are willing to learn to live in Him, our conscience will be full of feelings. We might feel that we have offended our parents or our siblings or that we have offended others by using their things. We might feel that we dress according to our preference and not according to the Lord's desire. Instead of ignoring such feelings, we should deal with them one by one. If we deal with them thoroughly, we will have peace in our conscience, and the Spirit will move more deeply in us. As long as we are willing to let Him move in us, more light will be manifested in us.

A Christian can be living and strong when his conscience is without offense. When our conscience has an offense, it becomes sick, and we cannot be strengthened in the Lord, nor can we testify before men. First Timothy 1:5 speaks of "love out of a pure heart and out of a good conscience and out of unfeigned faith." Our faith and love are linked to our conscience. Pure love, a good conscience, and unfeigned faith are related to one another. Without a good conscience, we cannot have pure love; rather, our love will not be pure. Furthermore, our faith will be weak; it will not be genuine or strong. When there is an offense in our conscience, there will be a leakage, our faith will leak away, and we will not be able to pray, because our conscience will condemn us. Since God is greater than our conscience, He will also condemn us. Hence, in order to have unfeigned faith and pure love, we must have a good conscience, a conscience without offense.

It is crucial for a believer to maintain a good conscience before the Lord. The apostle Paul says, "Holding faith and a good conscience, concerning which some, thrusting these away, have become shipwrecked regarding the faith" (v. 19). A person who thrusts away his conscience, that is, does not deal with the feeling of offense in his conscience, can be compared to a damaged ship that allows water to leak into it, causing it to be shipwrecked. When the conscience has a leaking hole, sinful things and worldly things will cause a believer to sink into the ocean of the world and into the abyss of sinful things. A person in this situation cannot be transcendent, cannot rise above sins and the world, and cannot live before God. Hence, a Christian must deal with his conscience until there is absolutely no offense in it. Then he will be like a ship without any leaks.

The apostle Paul said that he served God in a pure conscience (2 Tim. 1:3). Those who desire to fellowship with God, live before Him, and serve Him by taking Him as life must depend on the blood and the anointing. However, the continual application of the blood and the anointing depend on our dealing with our conscience. When we do not deal with our conscience, the cleansing of the blood will cease, and the anointing will also cease. Furthermore, our spiritual experiences will cease. Our spiritual dealings must begin with our conscience.

I hope that my words will touch your conscience and open a way for you. As those who have the life of God and who desire to live in Him and to take Him as life, we must take this way. When God moves in us, we will see light. This light will expose our sins, and as a result, our conscience will feel an offense. Then we should deal with our conscience; that is, we should confess our sin and deal with it. We must not be casual concerning this matter. If we do not deal with our conscience, we will not grow. When there is an offense in our conscience, our fellowship with God cannot be maintained, and we will not live in His presence. Hence, as soon as there is a feeling in our conscience, we must learn to deal with it immediately, confessing our sins to God. Sometimes we may also have to apologize to people and make restitution.

If we truly desire to grow in life and to experience the Lord as life, we must deal with our conscience until our conscience is very keen and responds even to a small mistake. Many saints deal with their conscience in a detailed way. When one saint went to visit a friend, he stood at the door because he was not invited into the house. He said, "The host did not ask me to come in. If I go in, I will violate his authority, and this would cause my conscience to lose its peace." When he entered into the living room, he would not sit down until the host asked him to. He said, "This house and this chair belong to the host; I am not the owner. If I sit down, I will violate his ownership." While in the living room, he dared not to pick up the newspaper and read it, because he was not the owner. If he had picked up the newspaper, he would have needed to confess to his host. This may sound like a joke, but we should all have experiences like this. This experience shows that this saint dealt with his conscience strictly; hence, his conscience was sharp and keen. If we are restricted by our conscience, our move and walk will not be careless.

Some people sit anywhere and touch anything they like without the permission of their host. They can even look at the things in the closets. This shows that they live in darkness. Their conscience does not have much feeling; hence, they cannot live in God. They move and walk freely according to their convenience. In John 7:6 the Lord Jesus said that His time was not ready, but with many people, their time is always ready. They enter when they want to, sit down when and where they want to, and touch what they want to. Such ones have not dealt with their conscience. Furthermore, some people are careless with their money; they think that if they owe a brother or sister, there is no need to take care of the debt in a full and accurate way. Such ones surely do not live in God or in the light, and the offenses in their conscience have not been dealt with properly.

If a person truly lives in God, the divine light in his conscience will restrain and restrict his walk. The divine light will manifest whether he is short in a matter or too much. It will also expose when he does something unnecessary and when he is improper. His conscience will be full of feelings. If he does not deal with these feelings, he will not be able to pray, he will not have the faith to pray, and he will not be able to fellowship with or to live in the Lord.

Whether we can enjoy the cleansing of the blood and the anointing depends on whether we are willing to deal with the offenses in our conscience. When God shines in us, our sins will be exposed, and our conscience will sense an offense. We should deal with this feeling immediately by applying the blood. When the blood cleanses us, the anointing ointment will anoint us with more of the element of God. This is the way that we grow. This cycle is not once for all. This cycle of the fellowship of life is unceasing. When the divine element is added to us, the divine light will become stronger. When the light is stronger, more sins will be exposed. When our sins are exposed, our conscience will condemn us. In order to deal with our conscience, we need the cleansing of the blood. It is through this cycle that we can experience the blood's cleansing and the anointing. As we experience the cycle of the fellowship of life, our naturalness will gradually decrease, and the divine element will gradually increase in us. This is the way to be delivered from the self, to live in God, and to let Him be our life.

CHAPTER NINE

PASSING THROUGH DEATH
TO LIVE OUT LIFE

Scripture Reading: John 12:24-26

In John 12:24-26 the Lord Jesus said, "Truly, truly, I say to you, Unless the grain of wheat falls into the ground and dies, it abides alone; but if it dies, it bears much fruit. He who loves his soul-life loses it; and he who hates his soul-life in this world shall keep it unto eternal life. If anyone serves Me, let him follow Me; and where I am, there also My servant will be. If anyone serves Me, the Father will honor him." According to the Lord's words, whoever hates his soul-life in this world will keep it unto eternal life. These verses speak of two lives: the soul-life, which is our human life, and the eternal life, which is God's life. If we love our soul-life and are not willing to let it pass through death, we will lose it. However, if we hate our soul-life in this age and allow it to be put to death, we will keep it unto eternal life. This is a serious matter. In verse 26 the Lord indicated that He was going to die, to pass through death; hence, those who followed Him also needed to die, to pass through death. The Lord as a grain of wheat fell into the ground and died; hence, the grains that have been brought forth in Him must also pass through death. Those who serve Him must also fall into the ground and die. The Lord entered into death; hence, we cannot serve the Him without falling into the ground and dying.

In the previous chapters we saw that God came to be our life. This emphasizes life. However, if there is life, there must be a living, because living is the outward expression of life. Hence, in this chapter we will fellowship concerning the expression of life, that is, our living. We will see how the divine life is lived out of us.

THE LAW OF DEATH

Everything in the universe operates according to its law. Living organisms have their respective law of life. Biology is the study of the law of various organisms. These laws are fixed and definite. If we want a certain life to live and grow, we must focus on its law.

Among the laws of life, there is the great law of death. Many Christians have an inaccurate understanding concerning the death of the Lord Jesus on the cross. In the Bible death has a negative aspect as well as a positive aspect. Whereas the negative aspect of death is perdition, the positive aspect includes more than redemption. Death is also the prerequisite for the divine life to grow in man. The death given to us by Adam is negative; this death comes from sin. If we have only the death from Adam, we will perish. However, we thank the Lord that He has given us another aspect of death. We treasure the cross because it is a symbol, a sign, of death. The cross of Calvary declares that a unique death has been accomplished in the universe. The salvation that we as Christians receive depends on this death.

Through the Lord's death on the cross, we have not only redemption but also life and the growth of life. Many of those who speak of the cross give the impression that the Lord's death on the cross was only for redemption; the Lord Jesus died on the cross to bear our sins, to be judged by God on our behalf, and to taste death for us. This is not wrong, but it is not complete. The Lord Jesus died on the cross not only to bear our sins and accomplish redemption; He died to release the divine life so that this life could grow in us and be lived out of us. This is what He said in John 12:24. The grain of wheat must die in order to become many grains. Such a death is not a terrible death; rather, it is a wonderful death, in which one grain of wheat became many grains. Such a death did not cause the grain of wheat to perish, but rather it released the life that was in the grain of wheat.

Without such a death on the cross, it would not be possible for the divine life within the Lord Jesus to be released. It was through His death that the life within Him could be released.

Hence, this death causes life to be released. The release of life through death is a great principle that applies to many organisms; if they do not pass through death, the life within them cannot be released. This is true not only with the plant life, such as a grain of wheat, but also with the animal life. In order for an egg to hatch and bring forth a baby chick, the eggshell must be broken. This breaking is the passing through death. Furthermore, in order for life to be transmitted from one organism to another, both parties need to pass through death. For example, in order to give blood, the donor must be pricked for blood to flow out, and the recipient must also be pricked in order for blood to flow in. This kind of pricking is in the principle of death. Not only so, the food that we eat, whether it is of the plant life or the animal life, also needs to pass through the principle of death. Anything that we eat must pass through death before it can enter into us to become nutrients. Similarly, God also passed through death before He could enter into us. If He had not passed through death, He would not have been able to enter into us to be our life.

THE LORD RELEASING HIS LIFE THROUGH DEATH

When the Lord Jesus died, we died with Him (Rom. 6:6). He was God clothed with humanity, and He died as God mingled with man. Hence, His death involved two parties: He passed through death in His humanity in the flesh, and we passed through death in His humanity. It is through such a death that His life could be released and imparted into us. It is through such a death that His life could be released to enter into innumerable people. This glorious fact was accomplished on the cross and is the gospel that we preach.

The gospel is that as a man, God has already accomplished what He wants to achieve in us. The gospel conveys to us the fact of His accomplishment. When a person receives the gospel, he confesses this fact, and the Holy Spirit accomplishes it in him. The content of the gospel is that God became flesh, put on humanity, was mingled with man, lived as a man on the earth, and died on the cross as a man. In His death both God and man died (Acts 20:28). Through this death the life within Him was released and imparted into man. He has accomplished this fact, and the gospel conveys it to us. When we believed in and acknowledged this gospel, the Spirit touched our inner being and fulfilled this fact in us.

THE DIVINE LIFE GROWING THROUGH DEATH

According to what the Holy Spirit has fulfilled in us, we were joined to God in His death, and we received Him as our life. These are facts. The life within us now needs to be expressed. This life flows out of God into us, and it must also flow out of us into others. The divine life will flow out of us in the same way that it entered into us. It entered into us through death, and it will flow out of us also through death. Death is the way of life. In order for life to flow, there must be death. If there is no death, life will not have the way to flow out or to flow in. Just as life needed death in order to flow out of God and enter into us, only through death can life flow out of us and enter into others. Death is the only gateway. For this reason, those who know life also treasure death, because if there is death, there is also life. If we desire to touch life, we must first touch death. If there is no death, there cannot be life. Simply speaking, no death, no life. This is a law. Life enters through death and flows out through death. Life was imparted into us through death and grows in us through death. Without death, life cannot enter, and without death, life cannot grow. This is a law.

Every time that life operates in us, it results in our being put to death. The operation of life always demands that we die; it puts us in death. If we consider our experience, we will see that whenever we consecrate ourselves to the Lord and are willing to respond to His demands by being a vessel and letting Him live in us, He gains more ground in us and operates a little more in us. When He operates, He asks us to cut off or forsake certain things. This cutting off and forsaking are according to the principle of death. God's only demand is that we die. By responding to His demand, we are agreeing to die. In other words, we are agreeing to pass through death by His life.

Suppose a brother is very close to a friend who is an unbeliever. The divine life within him may demand that he give up this friendship. If the brother's love for his friend is too strong, he may be reluctant to meet this demand. As a result, he will be in conflict with the life of God within him. The human life and the divine life have different tastes. The brother might feel that his friendship is very sweet, but the divine life says that this friendship is not sweet. These tastes are entirely different. When we were saved, we received God's life in addition to our human life. These two different lives, the human life and the divine life with their different natures and tastes, are now in us. For this reason, there is often a conflict within us.

It is difficult for a person to have two lives within him. The human life loves to make friends with the world, but God's life hates any friendship with the world. The human life is very irritable, but God's life is very gentle. When the human life says, "Hurry up! Hurry up!" the divine life says, "Slow down! Slow down!" We are in a hurry, but He is not; we want to run, but He does not move. Is this not difficult? This is our situation in small things and in our daily life. This is the situation of every believer. After we received God's life into us, there have been two lives in us. Hence, either we die, or He suffers. In order to live out the life of God, we must die. When we consecrate ourselves, we give God the opportunity to gain more ground in us and to live out of us. He is always requiring that we die. He requires that we cut off worldly friendships, that is, forsake our friends in the world. In principle, such a cutting off, such a forsaking, is to die.

HE WHO KEEPS HIS SOUL-LIFE LOSING IT, AND HE WHO LOSES HIS SOUL-LIFE KEEPING IT

If we are unwilling to respond to the demand of death by keeping our natural soul-life, we will lose our soul-life in this age and in the next age. Our human life cannot be lived out in a proper way when the divine life cannot be lived out of us. A Christian who desires to be proper, weighty, and noble must lose his soul-life. The more he loses his soul-life, the more weighty and noble it will become. A Christian who only cares for his soul-life and is unwilling to die will eventually lose his soul-life; not only will his life be base, but he will even become abnormal.

In order to be a weighty person, we must lose our soul-life. To be a proper, wise, and understanding person with proper and rich thoughts, abundant and appropriate emotions, and a discerning and thorough view in every situation, we must live according to the demand of God's life by putting our soul-life to death in every matter. The more we put our soul-life to death, the wiser and more understanding we will become. Not only so, our thoughts will be clearer, we will have insight, our discernment will be more accurate, and our emotions will be richer. This is a marvelous thing! But if we insist on keeping our soul-life, we will eventually have a weakened mind and unbalanced emotions.

Let us consider the matter of anger. According to the Bible, a Christian can be angry but not sin. Ephesians 4:26 says, "Be angry, yet do not sin." Hence, being angry is not always equivalent to sinning. The Bible permits us to be angry, but there should be a limitation to our anger; we should not become so angry as to sin. To be so angry that we hit someone with our fist is to be angry to the point of sinning. A person who can be angry and yet not sin has lost his soul-life. Such a person has a proper life and can be likened to a good car that can move as fast or slow as needed. Some people, however, are not like this. Either they do not move at all, or once they start moving, they cannot stop. When such a person is happy, he is in ecstasy; and when he is friendly, he is kind to the uttermost. But if there is a slight misunderstanding, he disputes heatedly. In contrast, a person with a proper life can be angry, but his anger quickly dissipates. The life of such a person is not only proper but also strong.

The proper way for the soul-life to be strong is to lose it. Those who lose their soul-life will keep it unto eternal life. Do not consider John 12:25 as something only for the future. Although eternity is included, the emphasis is that our own life will be kept unto God's life. The more our life is put to death by God's life, the more we will enter into His life. As a result, our life will be uplifted, strengthened, and transcendent; we will have a life that has passed through death and resurrection. Then whether or not we become angry, our emotions will be balanced. The result of putting our soul-life to death as a response to the demand of the divine life is that our life is saved and kept by entering into the divine life.

After a person is saved, he has two lives in him: the human life and the life of God. God wants us to live by His life. His life will put our life to death, because the divine life requires our human life to pass through death. If we preserve our own life and are not willing to let it pass through death, we will destroy and lose it. Eventually, our thoughts and discernment will become weak, and our emotions will become unbalanced. However, if we are willing to let the divine life put our life to death, if we are willing to lose our soul-life, our life in the divine life will be strong; we will have a strong mind, rich emotions, and proper discernment, having wisdom and insight. We will become transcendent, strong, and proper. We will not be strong gods but strong persons; we will be persons whose soul-life has passed through death and has resurrected in the divine life. In other words, through death the divine life is mingled with our life, and our nature is changed and strengthened. May all God's children learn this precious lesson and experience such a precious reality.

CHAPTER TEN

BEING CONFORMED
TO THE LORD'S DEATH

Scripture Reading: Phil. 3:10; 2 Cor. 4:7-12, 16-17

As a result of regeneration, every believer has two lives: the human life and God's divine life. Although we have two lives, God wants us to live only by His life. If God had not revealed this wonderful matter to us, we could not imagine that the God of the universe desires to be lived out of man. He intends to have a group of people who have the human life but live by His life. He earnestly desires that these people would allow Him to live out of them. This thought is mysterious and wonderful. God wants to be expressed, but He does not want to be expressed in Himself. He wants to enter into man and be expressed in man.

THE GREATEST PROBLEM TO TAKING GOD AS LIFE

God desires His divinity to be expressed in humanity. Such a thought does not exist in man. Man has the concept of morality, the concept of good and evil. People think that as long as they depart from evil and have a good, ethical living, they are noble persons. According to this view, human beings should be vessels of morality, expressing morality. However, this is not God's thought. He has no intention for man to be a vessel of morality, expressing merely morality and goodness. God desires man to be His vessel so that He can be contained in this vessel and expressed from this vessel.

Man is a living vessel; hence, it is rather difficult for God to enter into man to be man's life. This desire is not a simple matter. Here is a simple illustration, even though it is not adequate. It is easier to ask a simple person to accept the thoughts of a wise person than it is to ask a wise person to accept the thoughts of a foolish person. Nor is it easy to ask a smart person to accept the decisions of another smart person.

It is not so easy to put two lives together. If we did not have the human life, God would be free to put His life into us as He wishes, but He did not take this way. It pleases God to put Himself in the living creature that He created. Although our human life is weak, it is also obstinate, stubborn, opinionated, and self-willed. If we use human relationships as an example, it is hard to find a couple who have been together for ten years but have never argued. Some people may not fight with their fists, but they use their tongues to fight. It is hard to find a couple who get along all the time. Every person has a strong life. The wife does not submit to her husband, nor does the husband respect his wife. Two brothers may be able to live together, but this does not mean that they do not have issues. Some people might say that this is a matter of different opinions, but it is really a matter of different lives. When people have different lives, it is not so easy for them to get along.

Now let us consider this: God dwells in us as our life. Although our life is weak, we are rather strong. Hence, He encounters difficulties when He wants us to take Him as our life.

GENUINE LOVE AND SUBMISSION TO THE LORD DEPENDING ON TAKING HIM AS LIFE

A person who loves the Lord puts aside his soul-life and takes the Lord as his life. For example, a wife who loves her husband should take her husband's life as her life. If a husband loves his wife, he will take his wife's life as his life. However, we should not understand this word in a natural way; it is not that a husband should give up his life for his wife's sake. Rather, a husband who loves his wife will consider her when he speaks, acts, and makes decisions. A couple who have been together for forty or fifty years often look alike, because they are alike in their speaking, attitude, and taste. The wife resembles the husband, and the husband resembles the wife. The more they love each other, the more they will resemble each other. Similarly, if we love the Lord, we will put ourselves aside and take Him as our life, and as a result, we will become like Him.

Taking the Lord as our life touches God's heart more than doing many things for Him or accomplishing many works. We touch His heart when we put aside our life to take Him as life and to let Him be our life because we love Him. It is not that we do not have a life, but because of our love for Him, we continually deny our soul-life so that we do not live by our life but take His life. As a result, our living is not merely a matter of obeying Him or of doing things that please Him, but our living is God being expressed from within us.

In contacting the saints, we often feel that this brother is very good or that sister is very good, because they have many positive virtues. However, it is not so easy to smell the flavor of God in their virtues. Although these virtues come out of their human life, God is not expressed in these virtues. Some believers have done many prosperous and flourishing works for God, but these works do not bear the divine element. There are other saints, however, who do not have an outward display of many virtues or who seemingly have not accomplished anything of significance, but they bear the flavor of God and of His element. When we touch them, our first impression is not of their virtues but of God. God comes forth in their living and their work.

Such an expression of God is what makes the four Gospels different from books on ethics. The books of Confucius and other Chinese philosophers have an ethical flavor, but they do not bear the flavor of God. The Gospels are the biography of Jesus, the Nazarene. When we read His biography, we see that whether He was speaking, healing the sick, or casting out demons, He expressed God; God came forth from Him. Jesus was a man, but He took God as His life and lived by God. In His living and in His work, His actions were not focused on doing good or on accomplishing a great work. His focus was God. He let God live in Him and be expressed in Him.

It is true that the Lord obeyed God's will. But we must have a proper understanding of what this means. The Lord did not merely obey God's will, nor did He do things to please God apart from God. His obeying God's will transcended this level. He denied His life and lived by the divine life to obey the Father's will. In other words, His obeying of the Father's will was His letting the Father live out of Him. He fully cooperated with God by receiving God as life; He denied His life to live by the Father's life. The Lord did not only do things for God or work for God, but He let the Father live out of Him. He accomplished God's will not by doing the things that the Father ordained; rather, He accomplished God's will by letting the Father live from within Him. Such a living can be seen in His healing the sick, His casting out demons, and His teaching. Whatever He did was the Father living out from Him. This is what it means to do God's will, to obey God. When we deny our self, take God as life, let Him live in us, and live by His life, we are obeying God and doing His will.

THE SOUL-LIFE NEEDING TO DIE IN ORDER TO TAKE GOD AS LIFE

In order for God's life to be lived out of man, the soul-life must die. This is indicated by the baptism of the Lord Jesus. We surely need to be baptized when we repent and believe in the Lord, because we are sinners. But why did the Lord Jesus need to be baptized when He began His work (Matt. 3:13-17)? The Lord's baptism has many significances. His being baptized was a declaration to the whole universe that as a man He was willing to be put to death. He was not corrupt, nor was He sinful; He was without sin. But in order to do God's work, accomplish God's will, and live for God, He, even as a sinless man without corruption, needed to die. For this reason, He placed Himself into death through baptism.

The Lord Jesus continually put His life to death and let God live in Him. Hence, He lived out God. From the beginning of His ministry, He never left the position of death. This is how He served God in order that God could live out of Him.

We should not understand being in the place of death to mean suffering. The thought that the cross is a suffering is poison from Catholicism. It is true that there is suffering related to the cross, but suffering is not the main meaning of the cross. The Roman government would say that to put a person on the cross was to kill him. Hence, the focus of the cross is not suffering but death. Once a brother whose wife was sick said to another brother, "This is the cross that the Lord gave me.

How can I not bear it?" There was also a sister who could not find a suitable maid and was constantly looking for a new one. When she spoke with the saints about this matter, she said, "It is so hard to find a suitable maid. Nevertheless, I thank and praise the Lord for the cross that He gave me." Most of God's children regard the experience of the cross to be a matter of suffering.

However, the cross does not stress suffering but death. The purpose of the cross is not to make us suffer but to kill us. The Lord's baptism at the beginning of His ministry was a declaration in which He seemed to say, "As a man, I am standing in the place of death. I am serving God in death. It is not I, Jesus the Nazarene, who lives, but it is God who lives in Me. Although I have life, even a sinless life, I will not live by My human life. God wants to be My life, and He wants to live out of Me, so I want to take Him as My life. I put My life in the place of death; I am willing to hang on the cross. I will not come down from the cross so that God may live out of Me."

The dying of the Lord Jesus on the cross did not occur only at Golgotha. He lived a crucified life. From the beginning of His ministry, He chose the cross and He never left the position of the cross. In serving God by casting out demons, healing the sick, and preaching to the people, He stood in the death of the cross so that God could be lived out.

For this reason, when we read the Gospels, we see that God was manifested in Jesus the Nazarene. His words and His conduct were filled with God; His living and His work were the expression of God. He was Jesus the Nazarene, but He did not express or live out a Nazarene; He expressed and lived out the glorious God. He was a lowly man who expressed the glorious God. This is glorious!

God delights in such a living. This was the living of the Lord Jesus, and it should also be our living. We are lowly people, but God desires to live out of us. Hence, death is necessary. If we love Him and give ourselves to Him, He will operate in us, and we will sense that there is a demand in His operation that we die. Genuine obedience to Him involves the acceptance of death. Obedience without death is not genuine obedience. It is not necessary for us to be concerned about obeying Him, for genuine obedience is death. Every time that the Lord operates, He demands that we die. We should say, "Lord, I am willing to deny the self and be put to death, because I love You. You have already put me in death; I am willing to accept this fact. I accept what You have arranged and stand in what You have accomplished. Since I am already dead, how can I still be living? I accept this death." Obedience is not a problem when we accept God's demand of death. Genuine obedience is death.

Philippians 2:8 says that the Lord was obedient unto death. Unless we die, our obedience is not absolute and not genuine. Absolute and genuine obedience is the obedience unto death. Hence, it is not a matter of obedience but of death. Every demand that the Lord makes in us is a demand for us to die. If we are willing to die, we will have genuine obedience.

BEING CONFORMED TO THE LORD'S DEATH THROUGH THE BREAKING IN OUR ENVIRONMENT

It is not easy to speak of the truth and the experience of being put to death, because we are not like the Lord; He was always willing to stand in death. For this very reason God must raise up situations in our environment to deal with us. A person who desires to take the Lord as life cannot avoid the dealings from his environment; he should not expect his environment to be smooth. The more we seek the Lord, the more we should be prepared to be dealt with in our environment. People want to take the way of prosperity, but genuine Christians, those who are in God's hand, often do not have a smooth journey on the earth; they encounter many blows and much breaking. This is not God's mistreatment or His punishment; rather, this is because He loves us. He desires to live in us and to give Himself to us as our enjoyment, but there are many frustrations in us. Hence, when it is necessary, He uses our environment to deal with us so that we can be put to death. Our environment forces us to experience death.

Those who desire to follow the Lord, live by Him, take Him as life, and let Him live in them will not have an easy way. He knows our impurities and how much we live by our soul-life. Therefore, He stirs up our environment at appropriate times to touch certain matters and to put us to death. He uses our environment to put us to death in small things and in big things. The Holy Spirit not only operates to put us to death; He also rules over our environment to create a situation that compels us to die. Hence, we have the demand of death within and the compelling of death without; we must die.

We thank God that we have the Holy Spirit inwardly and our environment outwardly. The first half of Romans 8 speaks of the Holy Spirit, but the second half speaks of our environment. *All things work together for good to those who love God* refers to our being conformed to the image of God's Son; this is equivalent to taking God as life and expressing the image of God (vv. 28-29). The Spirit of life operates to make us sons of God. However, this is not enough. We also need outward matters and things in our environment to break us, to put us into the mold of the Lord's death.

The death of the Lord Jesus is a mold. This mold is to deny the self and let God live, to put the soul-life to death and live by God's life. The Holy Spirit uses all things and all matters in our environment to place us into the mold of the Lord's death. The longer we stay in this mold, the more we will be conformed to His death; we will deny the self, put our soul-life to death, and let God live out of us. Being conformed to the Lord's death is what Paul pursued (Phil. 3:10). As those who live in the Lord's death, we will bear the putting to death of Jesus in our body (2 Cor. 4:10). The death of the Lord Jesus does a work of killing in us through our environment, and the result is that the life of the Lord Jesus is lived out of us (v. 11).

THE BREAKING OF THE EARTHEN VESSEL
FOR THE MANIFESTING OF THE TREASURE WITHIN

In 2 Corinthians 4:7 the apostle Paul says that God's life in us is a treasure and that we are earthen vessels. Then in verses 8 and 9 he says that the apostles were pressed on every side, unable to find a way out, persecuted, and cast down. The purpose of such experiences from our environment is for the death of the Lord Jesus to do a killing and breaking work in us so that the treasure within will manifest its surpassing power. This power is the power of resurrection, not the power of creation. The result of this manifestation is life in others (v. 12).

Indeed, even though we are earthen vessels, it is not so easy for us to be broken. From one perspective, we are fragile, and it is easy for us to get into trouble and to be damaged. But from another perspective, we are rather hard, strong, and impregnable, and it may require a substantial blow to break us. Hence, God often uses things in our environment to strike us. It is not that God chastises or disciplines us because we are wrong. The concept of chastisement and discipline is according to law and ethics. Paul was much better than you and me, but his suffering was worse than ours. It is not that God disciplined Paul severely and now disciplines us lightly. Nor is it that we need less discipline than Paul did. The purpose of the striking in our environment is entirely for God, the treasure, to manifest His surpassing power, His glorious life, from within us. Even though our outer man is decaying, our inner man is being renewed day by day (v. 16); the treasure within us is being manifested more from day to day. The momentary lightness of our affliction is working out for us, more and more surpassingly, an eternal weight of glory (v. 17). This glory is the manifestation of God, the maturity of His life, and the manifestation of resurrection power. In order for this glory to be manifested, we must pass through all kinds of sufferings. May God have mercy upon us so that we would see that we need to die in order for God to be our life.

CHAPTER ELEVEN

DYING TO LAW AND LIVING TO GOD

Scripture Reading: Gal. 2:19-20; Phil. 1:20-21; Rom. 7:4, 6

In Galatians 2:19-20 Paul says, "I through law have died to law that I might live to God. I am crucified with Christ; and it is no longer I who live, but it is Christ who lives in me; and the life which I now live in the flesh I live in faith, the faith of the Son of God, who loved me and gave Himself up for me." These two verses cover God's redemption. In this chapter we will focus on verse 19, which speaks of dying to law and living to God. In order to experience God as life, a Christian must know what it is to die to law and what it is to live to God.

GOD'S ETERNAL INTENTION AND
THE CREATION OF MAN

God's eternal intention is to enter into man to be man's life. This thought was in God's heart in eternity past, before He created the heavens and the earth. God in the Son and as the Spirit wants to enter into man to be man's life and to be mingled with man as one. He wants to be man's content, and He wants man to express Him. This is the intention that God ordained in eternity past.

Creation was the first step that God took in fulfilling His intention. God created the universe and all things in it, and then He created man as a vessel for His expression. His creation of man differs from His creation of other living creatures. He did two particular things when He created man. First, He made man in His own image and according to His own likeness (Gen. 1:26). He made man so that he would be suitable for His expression. If we want to make a vessel, we should first consider the purpose and the goal of the vessel before deciding on the shape of the vessel. Furthermore, we should consider whether the vessel would contain a solid or a liquid. This was how God created man. He made man in His image and according to His likeness so that man would be suitable to contain and express Him.

The second particular thing that God did was to form a human spirit within man (Zech. 12:1). This is the biggest difference between man and all other creatures. Eagles and monkeys are agile, but they do not have a spirit. Lions and tigers are fierce and powerful, but they do not have a spirit. Elephants and whales are much bigger than man, but they do not have a spirit. Man is special because he has a human spirit. Hence, man is the highest organism on the earth because he has a human spirit, not because he is more nimble, more powerful, bigger, or taller than other organisms.

The human spirit is a special organ entirely for contacting and receiving God. In order to contact something, we must use the appropriate organ. Just as God created man with a stomach in order for man to receive food, He also created man with a spirit in order for man to contact and receive Him. If we did not have a stomach, we would be unable to digest food. Similarly, God created us with a human spirit in order for us to receive Him.

Culture and education neglect the human spirit. Physical education deals with the physical body and is in the realm of the body. Intellectual education deals with the mind, and moral education largely deals with ethical choices related to our will. Both intellectual and moral education are in the realm of the soul. There is, however, no aspect of education that focuses on the human spirit. Even religion merely cultivates man's soul. Religion does not touch the human spirit. We must understand that our relationship with God is in our spirit. It is a relationship of the spirit. God created us with a human spirit so that by means of this spirit we may contact Him and receive Him.

Man possesses God's image and God's likeness, and he has the capacity to contain God for His expression. This is possible because God created a receiving organ in man so that man might receive Him. Thus, God is able to enter into man and to be expressed through man. These are the preparatory steps that God took when He created man.

MAN'S CHOICE AND HIS FALL

After creating man, God placed man in front of the tree of life (Gen. 2:8-9). The tree of life signifies God coming to be life to man. God desired to enter into man, but instead of appearing to man as the glorious and great God, He presented Himself as the tree of life, having no display of honor or glory, as food in order to be eaten by man. Many people think that God always manifests Himself in a splendid and majestic manner. However, this is not the way that He presented Himself to man. He humbled Himself, presenting Himself as the tree of life in order to be food to man. The Lord Jesus came to the earth in the same way. He did not come in splendor or majesty; rather, He humbly said, "I am the living bread which came down out of heaven" (John 6:51). He was so humble and accessible that even little children were not afraid to come to Him (Matt. 19:13-14). God placed man before the tree of life, showing that His intention was to be food for man in order to be man's life.

God also wanted to let man know that there was a problem in the universe. God had an adversary, an enemy, who was contending and struggling with Him. Everything that this enemy did was with the intention of destroying God's work. Hence, in addition to the tree of life, God caused the tree of the knowledge of good and evil to also grow (Gen. 2:9). God then warned man that the result of contacting this tree is death (v. 17; Rom. 5:12). The tree of the knowledge of good and evil refers to Satan. Satan can give man only the knowledge of good and evil. Satan is the tree of knowledge, which is related to good and evil. He is also the result of receiving mere knowledge; that is, he is the tree of death. On one side, there is the tree of life, which only involves life. On the other side, there is another tree, which involves the knowledge of good and evil and results in death. God presented Himself as food for man to eat, and Satan also wanted to enter into man. Satan imitates God in everything that He does. Sometimes Satan goes ahead of God to imitate what God will do. God has such an enemy.

Hence, when God put the tree of the knowledge of good and evil in the garden of Eden, He warned the man whom He had created, saying, "Of every tree of the garden you may eat freely, but of the tree of the knowledge of good and evil, of it you shall not eat; for in the day that you eat of it you shall surely die" (Gen. 2:16-17). This word was not only a command but also a warning.

God gave man two choices in order to manifest that He is great. God does not want to force His will on man. The use of such force would not be pleasant. God was pleased to let the man, whom He had created, exercise his free will to choose God. It pleases God for man to choose Him according to his own will. This is also a great shame to Satan. If God had forced man to receive Him, Satan could have accused God, saying, "You forced Yourself into man. That was not the voluntary choice of Your creature." By not forcing man to receive Him, God sealed Satan's mouth. God intended to show Satan that man has absolute freedom and self-will. Man can make choices according to his will. When God placed man between the tree of life and the tree of the knowledge of good and evil, He gave man the opportunity to choose between Himself and Satan. Man had the opportunity to eat either of the tree of life or of the tree of the knowledge of good and evil, that is, to choose God or Satan. Furthermore, God told man that the result of choosing Satan was death.

God was willing to wait for man to choose Him, but Satan could not wait. Satan came in quickly to do something, to seduce, steal, and lure man away from God. Man was seduced by Satan to eat the fruit from the tree of the knowledge of good and evil and thus received Satan (3:1-6). As a result, man had three problems related to sin. First, he committed a sinful deed. Second, he now had a record of sin before God. Third, Satan's sinful nature entered into man; thus, man possesses the evil nature of Satan. This evil nature is called sin (singular), as in Romans 6 through 8. Within man there is something living called sin. Our outward behavior, our sins, come out of the inward nature of sin that was injected into us by Satan. Satan poisoned us by injecting sin into us. As a result, we have a sinful nature, which produces many sinful deeds.

GOD BECOMING THE SECOND MAN

It seemed that the man whom God created for Himself was destroyed by Satan. Man has a record of sin before God, and he has sinful deeds without and a sinful nature within. Man, seemingly, is completely lost. However, God would not stop. It does not matter what His enemy does; God will carry out His intention. Hence, He became flesh and put on the human nature to be a man. God did not enter into humanity in an ordinary way. He was begotten in a virgin by the Holy Spirit. Although He was a genuine man, possessing human nature, He was not contaminated with the sin of the flesh (Rom. 8:3; 2 Cor. 5:21; Heb. 4:15). He had a human body with its human nature, but He was not contaminated by the sin within the fallen human nature.

God entered into humanity to be a man. First Corinthians 15:47 calls Him the second man. Adam and his descendants are included in the first man. The first man, Adam, was injected with the poison of sin, and he has sinful deeds and a record of sin before God. Every man is included in the first man. When the first man sinned, all men were constituted sinners (Rom. 5:18-19). No matter what a person's age may be, he has been sinning for six thousand years in Adam. When Adam sinned, all men sinned.

The Bible has a wonderful way of calculating matters concerning man. According to Hebrews 7:9-10, when Abraham gave one-tenth of the spoil to Melchizedek, the king of Salem, Levi, an offspring in the loins of Abraham, was paying tithes as well. While Abraham was offering tithes, his fourth-generation descendant was also offering tithes. This is the way the Bible calculates matters concerning man. In the same principle, when Adam sinned, all his descendants sinned with him. Hence, the entire adamic race has received the poison of Satan, has committed sinful deeds, and has a record of sin. The first man, including all of us who are in him, is completely defiled.

Then God came. He put on human nature, had a human body, and possessed the form of a man. God became a man. He is the second man. The second man is joined to the first man, but He does not have the sinful nature of the first man. This is wonderful.

According to 1 Corinthians 15:45, God became "the last Adam." The first Adam was created by God, but God Himself became the second man and the last Adam. One was a matter of creation, and the other was a becoming. These two men are joined to each other in their outward physical form and in their inward God-created human nature but not in the sinful nature. The second man had the likeness of the flesh of sin but not the sinful nature. Thus, in the second man the Creator is mingled with created man.

THE TEST OF THE LAW

Before becoming a man, God used various ways over a period of four thousand years to expose man, showing him that he is corrupt, sinful, evil, and unable to save himself. During this time, the law was the last means that God used to test and to prove man so that man would know that he is sinful, corrupt, and utterly unable to overcome sin.

Seemingly, God wanted man to keep the law, but this was not His intention. This part of the Old Testament is difficult to understand. In Exodus, Leviticus, Numbers, and Deuteronomy there are many words that require man to keep the law. God seemed to say, "If you keep the law, you will be blessed, but if you break the law, you will be cursed." Such words suggest that God wanted man to keep the law. However, if we touch the spirit of the Old Testament, we will see that God had no intention for man to keep the law. He knew that man could not keep the law. He knew that man would break the law and violate it, but He used the law to show man his wicked, evil, and hopeless inward condition. The law can be compared to a mirror that enables a person to see his condition. Parents know that children like to play in the dirt. A child's face might be covered with dirt, but he will not acknowledge that he is dirty. The best way for parents to show a child that he needs to be washed is to give the child a mirror. As soon as the child looks in the mirror, he will understand that he needs to be washed. There is no need for an adult to give any explanation. The law is a mirror to expose man's sins. Regrettably, when man receives the law, he mistakenly thinks that God wants him to obey the law. Therefore, man tries his best to obey the law. However, the more he tries, the more he fails. The more he tries to not break the law, the more he breaks it. Through God's use of the law, man is convinced, subdued, and silenced.

THE SIGNIFICANCE OF
THE LORD'S LIVING ON THE EARTH

God became a man. The Lord Jesus was a genuine man possessing the human life and nature. However, He possessed not only the human life but also the divine life; that is, He had God with His human life. The Lord did not live by His human life but by God's life. He lived only before God and in God, and He took God as His life. He did not care for the law and never placed Himself solely under the obligation of the law. This does not mean that He violated the law. His living not only met the requirement of the law but even fulfilled and complemented that which was lacking in the law (Matt. 5:17). Nevertheless, there was no sense that He was merely keeping the law; rather, He was expressing God. While the Lord Jesus was on earth, He did not live by His life but by taking God as life. Furthermore, He was obligated not merely to the law but to God. He did not live merely under the law; He lived in God. The Lord's living was not the life of a man keeping the moral standard of the law. His living was an expression of God; God was manifested in His living.

The living of the Lord Jesus on the earth was a model, showing how all human beings should live. A proper person should deny the self and live by taking God as life and by letting God live in him. Furthermore, a proper person should not be obligated to anything except to God. This was the living of the man Jesus, as shown in the Gospels. God desires to work this model into His people so that they may, like the Son, deny their soul-life, take God as life, and be obligated only to God, not to the law. God wants to work this model into us.

THE ACCOMPLISHMENT
OF THE LORD'S REDEMPTION

For the fulfillment of God's desire, the Lord Jesus had to accomplish a few matters. First, the Lord had to solve the problem of man's sinful deeds and the problem of man's record of sin before God. Second, He had to terminate the corrupt, sinful nature in order to work Himself as the model into man. Third, He had to destroy Satan. Fourth, He had to solve the problem of the world, which hangs on Satan and usurps man.

These matters were dealt with through the crucifixion of the Lord Jesus. First, He bore our sins on the cross (1 Pet. 2:24; 2 Cor. 5:21); God caused the iniquity of us all to fall on Him (Isa. 53:6; John 1:29), and in Him God judged sin in the flesh (Rom. 8:3). Thus, His blood redeems us from our sins, solving the problems of our sinful deeds and our record of sin. Second, the Lord Jesus was crucified in the flesh; hence, man's sinful nature was put to death on the cross (v. 3). Third, He destroyed Satan, who is mixed with man's sinful nature (Heb. 2:14). Fourth, He judged the world, which hangs upon Satan (John 12:31; 16:11). On the negative side, these matters were solved by the Lord Jesus through His death on the cross.

Furthermore, on the positive side, through His death on the cross, the Lord released His divine life. The divine life is rich and includes many elements. This life was released through His death (12:24). Then He was resurrected to become the life-giving Spirit (1 Cor. 15:45) in order to give us life. Hence, everything has been accomplished. Our problems have been resolved, and the divine life has been released. Moreover, the Lord with all His riches is now the life-giving Spirit. This Spirit has been sent forth into all the earth. Hence, no matter where a person may be, when his heart turns to God—he confesses his sins and receives the redemption of the Lord Jesus— the Spirit will enter into him and apply to him everything that the Lord Jesus has accomplished, including the record of sins being removed, the problems of man's sinful deeds and sinful nature being resolved, Satan being terminated, and the world being judged. Not only so, such a one also receives the divine life of God.

Everything that the Lord accomplished through His death on the cross is in the Spirit. Therefore, when we let the Spirit have the ground to operate in us freely, He will lead us to experience all that the Lord has accomplished. We will experience our sins being forgiven, the record of our sins being cleansed, our sinful nature being put to death, and both Satan and the world being nullified. These items will be judged; they will no longer have any ground or authority in us. The Lord's death will do a continual work of eliminating these items in us. We will also experience God becoming our life to uplift our humanity so that we become people mingled with God.

THE RESULT OF LIVING TO LAW BEING FAILURE

God's way of salvation is to mingle with us. This should be our living. However, many of us still do not know God's way of salvation, nor do we see our weaknesses and impotence. Thus, we are still trying to keep the law. As a result, we fail repeatedly and are unable to experience the freedom and release in God's salvation.

This was also the experience of the apostle Paul. Before he was saved, he kept the law in Judaism and lived to the law. He did not know that man was corrupt, weak, and unable to keep the law. In Romans 7 he says that when he tried to keep the law that says, "You shall not covet," coveting of every kind was activated within him (vv. 7-8). Then he received revelation from the Lord to understand that though the law is good, man is corrupt; hence, because of the weakness of man, the law cannot accomplish anything (vv. 12, 14, 18, 10). Eventually, Paul realized that God does not deal with people according to the law but that God deals with people according to Himself (8:2-4). God has given Himself to us to be our life. He does not want us to live according to the law but to live in Him. He gave the law to test and prove man so that we would see that we are corrupt and weak. We cannot keep the law, and God never intended for us to keep the law. Hence, the law is not the way that God deals with man. God deals with man by giving Himself to man, entering into man as life, living in man, and living out many virtues, such as goodness, holiness, love, and righteousness.

Having such a realization, Paul could say, "I through law have died to law that I might live to God" (Gal. 2:19). This means that he had cut off his relationship with the law and did not pay attention to the requirements of the law. The law says, "You shall not covet" (Rom. 7:7; Exo. 20:17), but Paul knew that it was not a matter of coveting but a matter of dying to the law so that he could live to God. The law says, "You shall love your neighbor as yourself" (Matt. 19:19). Paul knew that he had died to this law and that he was living to God. This means that God was his life; Paul followed God and was responsible to God. If God said, "Paul, you should love your neighbor as yourself," Paul could reply, "Yes, God, but I cannot do it. You must live in me and live out of me by loving my neighbor." Hence, Paul did not live by his soul-life; he lived by God.

We need to be clear concerning the difference between living to law and living to God. Many preachers say that believers should be humble and meek, should obey their parents, and should be nice. These are laws. Christians who receive such teachings are like the Israelites at the base of Mount Sinai; they said, "All that Jehovah has spoken we will do" (Exo. 19:8). This is almost always the condition of Christians who pursue the Lord; they live to the law.

The result of living to the law is failure. If we are determined to be humble and exert much effort to be humble, we will eventually be proud. Even if we are not proud outwardly, we will be proud inwardly; we are not able to be humble. Similarly, we cannot keep any commandment in the Bible. Eventually, we will be like Paul, who cried out, "Wretched man that I am! Who will deliver me from the body of this death?" (Rom. 7:24). Hence, we need to see that if we live to the law, we will be miserable. If we know God as life, we will have the attitude of dying to the law, not of living to the law. We have come to grace, to Mount Zion (Heb. 12:22); we have died to law. We do not know how to be humble or patient, nor do we know how to honor our parents. We only know that God is life in us, we live by Him, and we live to Him. We do not know the law. We know God as life.

THE RESULT OF LIVING TO GOD
BEING TO OVERCOME

Only those who live to God can honor their parents, and only those who live in God can be humble. Such honoring of one's parents is not an outward behavior but the living out of

God. Similarly, such humility is not manufactured by man; it is the living out, the expression, of God.

Our determination is futile; it is useless to have regulations. We must die to law. God is in us. We do not need to make up our mind, to determine, or to have regulations; we only want God to live in us. Hence, we must find some time daily to read His Word, touch Him, receive Him, and maintain our fellowship with Him so that He lives in our every word and action. We live in Him, and He lives in us. Then we will not need the law; instead, God will live out many virtues in us.

Furthermore, Galatians 2:19-20 will be realized in us. We will know what it is to die to law and live to God. We have been redeemed, and the all-inclusive Spirit of life has entered into us. All that needs to die in us must be terminated and cut off so that the divine life can enter in and enliven us. The things that need to be cut off, put to death, and terminated include not only the record of sin, sinful deeds, the sinful nature, Satan, and the world but also the law. The law was given by God to expose man's condition, but man uses it for his expression. We should no longer live to the law or keep the law. We should live to God and let Him live in us.

Galatians 2:20 says, "I am crucified with Christ." We have been terminated, crucified. Hence, we are not under the law and do not have to keep the law; rather, we have died to the law. It is no longer we who live, but it is Christ who lives in us so that we may live to God, take Him as our life, and let Him live in us. Hence, we only know to love God, fellowship with Him, live in Him, and let Him live in us. We do not know the law or regulations; we know only to follow God, cooperate with Him, and coordinate with Him. We should always say Amen to His move in us, and we should cooperate with His operation in us. We should take Him as our life, live by Him, and let Him live in us. We must deny our soul-life. We are not obligated to any regulation, because we live to God. We are vessels of God. He has entered into us to be our life, and He wants us to live by Him and take Him as our life. We simply need to love Him and give ourselves to Him to live by Him, coordinate with Him, cooperate with His operation, live in Him, and let Him live in us.

The normal Christian life is according to the Lord's words in John 14:19: "Because I live, you also shall live." We live in the Lord, and the Lord lives in us. In such a living we can say, "Christ will be magnified in my body, whether through life or through death," and "to me, to live is Christ" (Phil. 1:20-21).

Galatians 2:19-20 and then Philippians 1:20-21 bring in the proper environment. These verses tell us what kind of person Paul was. He learned how to die to law and to everything outside of God, and he learned to live to God and to let God live in him. He was clear that he was crucified with Christ and that he no longer lived but that Christ lived in him. Therefore, God raised up environments to prove him. Some environments were unto life, and some were unto death. But whether the environment was of life or of death, everything was an opportunity for Christ to be magnified in Paul. He magnified Christ, lived by Christ, and took Christ as life. The result of such proving was that to Paul to live was Christ. This is the proper Christian life.

CHAPTER TWELVE

THE CORPORATE ASPECT
OF EXPERIENCING GOD AS LIFE

Scripture Reading: Eph. 3:16-19; 2 Tim. 2:22

In this chapter we will fellowship concerning another aspect of experiencing God as life. Experiencing God as life is not only an individual matter; it is also a corporate matter. God wants to be life not only to an individual believer but also to all those who believe into His Son. As those who have been saved, we have God in us as life. If we experience Him as life merely by ourselves, our experience will be very limited. Our experience of God as life is mainly through the experiences of other believers.

Every saved person is a member of the Body of Christ (Rom. 12:5). A member of our physical body often can enjoy the benefits of our body only through the other members. Similarly, under normal conditions a believer does not enjoy God as life only by himself. An isolated brother who enjoys God as life will gradually realize that his enjoyment does not last long and that his experience is limited. In order to experience God as life, we should pay attention not only to our individual experiences but also to the experiences of other believers. This is the corporate aspect of experiencing God as life.

APPREHENDING CHRIST WITH ALL THE SAINTS

Ephesians 3:18 says that we need to apprehend the dimensions of Christ—His breadth, length, height, and depth—with all the saints. We apprehend the dimensions of Christ with all the saints because no one can apprehend all the riches of Christ alone. No one can apprehend or grasp by himself the breadth, length, height, and depth of Christ.

Christ is immeasurable, just as the breadth, length, height, and depth of the universe cannot be measured. There is no way to measure the length of the universe. Likewise, we cannot describe how high is the height. There are high-rise buildings in Hong Kong and in New York City, but there is still quite a distance between the top of those buildings and the sky. They are not as high as the sky. Likewise, we cannot measure the breadth or depth of the universe.

Ephesians 3 says that when the saints experience Christ together, they can apprehend the breadth, length, height, and depth. The breadth, length, height, and depth refer to Christ. This is the only portion in the Bible that speaks of Christ in relation to the dimensions of the universe. The breadth of the universe is Christ, the length is Christ, the depth is Christ, and the height is also Christ. The breadth, length, height, and depth are Christ. He is immeasurable and unlimited; we cannot exhaust Him. When the apostle Paul wrote of the unlimitedness of Christ, he could not find more suitable words. According to verses 17 through 19, when Christ makes His home in our hearts, we will be filled unto all the fullness of God. Apprehending the unlimited fullness of God requires all the saints. Each of us can touch only a little of this fullness, just as a bucket cannot hold all the water in the ocean. Not only so, our personal experience is not independent; it is our experience with all the saints. The more we experience Christ, the more we will feel that we need to apprehend and experience Him with all the saints. We cannot experience Christ by ourselves; we must experience Him together with others.

NEEDING TO FIND SPIRITUAL COMPANIONS

The best way for the young brothers and sisters to experience Christ is to find at least two or three companions in the Lord. This is spoken of in 2 Timothy 2:22, which says, "Flee youthful lusts, and pursue...with those who call on the Lord out of a pure heart."

The Bible contains many examples of companions. There are many spiritual companions in the Old Testament. Caleb and Joshua were companions who followed God together (Num. 32:12). David and Jonathan were also spiritual companions

(1 Sam. 18:1). When Daniel was taken to Babylon, he had three friends who feared God and lived in His presence (Dan. 1:6). When Daniel encountered difficulties, they prayed together in one accord. Thus, their prayer was powerful and received the Lord's specific answer.

The principle of companions also exists in the New Testament and is strengthened. When the Lord Jesus sent out His disciples, they went in groups of two (Luke 10:1). This is the principle of companions. In the book of Acts the disciples rarely moved or acted alone. When Peter went out, John was with him (3:1). When Paul went out, Barnabas, Silas, Timothy, and Luke were his companions (12:25; 17:10; 20:4; 2 Tim. 4:11).

THE BENEFITS OF HAVING SPIRITUAL COMPANIONS

The best way to have spiritual growth and receive spiritual benefit is to find a few brothers and sisters to be our spiritual companions so that we can open to one another, seek one another, help one another, and solve one another's problems in all spiritual things. On one hand, we should regularly seek the Lord on our own, and on the other hand, with a pure heart we should frequently have open fellowship with a few brothers and sisters. We would be blessed if we would fellowship concerning our weaknesses or problems, concerning matters that we cannot overcome, and concerning matters that cause us to fall. We often cannot overcome a certain sin alone, but if we are willing to fellowship about it, the sin will be overcome. This is quite marvelous.

Suppose a young brother is having trouble understanding the Lord's leading concerning a certain matter. He can invite a few brothers over and fellowship with them about the problem. From our experience we know that he can become clear even while he is speaking. If he does not fellowship, he will not be able to understand the Lord's leading, but once he begins to speak, he often will become clear before the brothers even respond. The brothers have helped him, because without them, he would have no one to fellowship with, and he would not become clear. It is because he has people to fellowship with that he is able to understand the Lord's leading.

Suppose we are weak and do not have any joy. We might

not be able to rise above this situation no matter how much we pray. This is when we should find some brothers with whom to fellowship. The topic of our conversation may not be important, but after the conversation, we will be refreshed and uplifted.

Spiritual companions are such a great benefit because of the principle of the Body. God is our life, but He is not only in us individually; He is in us corporately. Therefore, whenever we fellowship, we will be helped by the other members, and they will be helped by us.

In order to kindle wood in a stove, there must be at least three pieces of firewood. It is very difficult to start a fire with only one piece of firewood, and if a fire is started, it will easily be quenched. This is an example of our condition before God. In order to pursue the Lord in a good way, we must find three to six brothers and sisters with whom we can come together regularly. We should be open and fellowship with one another without any reservation concerning our condition toward the Lord and our situation before Him. If we would practice this, our weaknesses will be swallowed up, our problems will be solved, the light in us will become brighter, our spirit will be strengthened and refreshed, and our love for the Lord will be more fervent. The benefits of having spiritual companions are too great.

Since there are so many benefits to having spiritual companions, all the young saints should find a few brothers or sisters to be their spiritual companions. Without such friends, their condition before the Lord will be hazardous, and many problems will arise. Therefore, they must have friends so that they can be balanced and steady. Some people are loners; they do not like to have friends. The more they are inclined to be alone, the more necessary it is for them to have friends, because friends will help them be more open. Some brothers and sisters were the only child in their family and were spoiled in their youth. As a result, they have a closed temperament and a secluded disposition, which greatly hinder their Christian life. The only way to remove this tendency of being closed and secluded is to have a few companions. Then such a brother will become one among many brothers, and such a sister will become one among many sisters. This will deliver them from being closed and secluded. In order to be broken, to be delivered from the self, and to become open instead of closed, we must have companions. Regardless of what we do, in ourselves we are closed and have no way to be open. We need companionship with some brothers and sisters in order to be open.

PRINCIPLES FOR FINDING SPIRITUAL COMPANIONS

There are several principles that we must take heed to when we are looking for companions.

Looking for Saved Ones

First, you should not seek companions among unbelievers (2 Cor. 6:14-18). Christians who seek friendship with unbelievers will eventually suffer a loss. An unbeliever can be likened to a person wearing dirty clothes, and a believer can be likened to a person wearing clean white clothes. By spending time together, the person in white clothes will eventually become dirty. We should not be quick to become companions with an unbeliever. Instead, we should preach the gospel to him and lead him to salvation so that he may become a brother in the Lord. Only then should we become his companion, because he would have put off his dirty clothes and put on clean white clothes.

Looking for Those Who Can Be of Mutual Help

Second, we should look for brothers and sisters who can be of mutual help; either they can help us, or we can help them. The purpose of seeking companions is so that we may know more of Christ and let Him live in us. Hence, we should not make friends with those who enjoy the world's pleasures, because instead of helping us to live in Christ, they will pull us to follow Satan and to take him as our life. We must pay attention to this point when we look for companions.

Looking for Three Kinds of Companions

Third, we should look for three kinds of companions. The first kind should be those who are at our spiritual level. This kind of friend is for mutual help—we can help him, and he can help us. The second kind should be more experienced in the Lord; he can lead us. We need to listen to such a one and receive his help, be restricted by him, and even be subject to him. I believe that Paul was such a companion to Timothy and to Titus; Paul was like their father. For this reason, Timothy and Titus had to learn submission, and they had to subject themselves to his authority (1 Tim. 1:1-2; Titus 1:4). We should also look for this kind of companion. The third kind of companion should be one who is younger and weaker. We should render him help and lead him like a big brother leading his younger siblings.

We should have these three kinds of companions. It is best for every believer to have two companions who are at the same level, a companion who is younger, and a companion who is older. The brothers should look for companions among the brothers, and the sisters should look for companions among the sisters. They should look for all three kinds of companions.

CAUTIONS CONCERNING
LOOKING FOR SPIRITUAL COMPANIONS

We would like to fellowship some more with regard to the cautions one should heed when looking for companions.

Fearing God

When the young brothers or sisters become companions, they must learn to fear God. We should never become so familiar with one another that we become loose, saying things or doing things that show no fear for God.

Respecting One Another

Under the fear of God, companions should also respect one another. We should avoid jesting and being loose because of familiarity. Being careless in our speech and our actions, such that the fear of God and our mutual respect are missing, will open a big door for Satan. Not only the young ones but even the older believers should not become relaxed concerning these two points. When I am with brothers and sisters and notice some kind of looseness, I immediately shut the door by becoming serious. It is right to be friends, but we should neither sacrifice the fear of God nor lose our respect for one another. If at any time we become so familiar with a particular companion that we lose the fear of God and become wild, loose, or relaxed, we should stop immediately and cut off that companionship. We must be on guard. I have a very intimate friend who went to be with the Lord. Having been friends for twenty years, we knew each other very well, understood one another, and were in one accord. However, the Lord can testify that when we were together, we did not jest. Sometimes we might say a few words of humor, but we never engaged in frivolous, irreverent, self-indulgent, or careless speaking. We always had an atmosphere of fearing God. For this reason, for twenty years our friendship did not have any problems. I wrote the hymn "Rest in the Lord" when he passed away. We came to know each other after we were saved. I chose him as my companion, and he also chose me as his companion. For twenty years we walked before the Lord together. Our friendship gave us only benefits because we did not lose our fear of God; instead of being loose, we always respected each other.

Rejecting Natural Affection

We should also guard against having natural affection, natural love. As companions in the Lord, we should love one another, but we should kill any natural affection. Natural affection is to be excessive in our love for one another. Natural affection is harmful, and it offends the Lord. We should love one another in the Lord, but we should not bring in any natural affection.

It is rather difficult to love without having natural affection. However, if we cannot restrain ourselves in this matter, our friendship will become a trap, and we will become loose. Anyone who cannot restrain his natural affection is also an unrestrained person before the Lord. We should be strict and restrained before the Lord in order to love our brother but reject natural affection. This also applies to the sisters. The sisters should love one another, but they should be restrained and not exercise natural affection. Friendship in the church is different from friendship in the world. People in the world love others in the realm of natural affection. But having more natural affection than love is often harmful. The brothers or sisters should love one another without natural affection. Our love must be in the Lord without any natural human affection. If we can know the difference between love in the Lord and natural affection and can guard against the exercise of natural affection, our companionships will be profitable, and we will not incur any loss.

PURSUING TOGETHER WITH SPIRITUAL COMPANIONS

I hope that the young saints will find three to five spiritual companions among the brothers and sisters in order to pursue the Lord together. On one hand, we should fear God and respect one another, and on the other hand, we should love one another and forsake natural affection. It is good to come together often in order to fellowship, pray, read the Lord's Word, and learn spiritual lessons together. When we encounter difficulties or problems, we should bear one another and solve the problems together. Then our living will be according to the principle of the Body. The results and the benefits of such a living are unlimited. The breadth, length, height, and depth of Christ, His unlimited fullness, will be opened to us and will flow unceasingly into us. Furthermore, we will grow speedily in a balanced and steady way.

CHAPTER THIRTEEN

THE RELATIONSHIP BETWEEN
GOD BEING LIFE TO MAN
AND THE BUILDING OF THE CHURCH

Scripture Reading: 1 Cor. 3:9, 16-17; 10:16; 12:12-13; 1 Tim.
3:15; 1 Pet. 2:4-5

THE ISSUE OF GOD BEING LIFE TO MAN
BEING HIS HABITATION

God's ultimate goal in being life to man and in mingling
with man is to have a habitation. According to the Bible, God's
work does not only consist of creation and redemption. His
work includes His entering into man to live in man as life and
to build the church as His habitation. As the result of His
work, He will obtain a habitation—the holy city, New Jerusalem, which is depicted at the end of the Bible (Rev. 21:2, 10).
Bible readers admit that the New Jerusalem is the ultimate
and highest result of God's work. The New Jerusalem is God's
habitation in the universe; it is where He can settle down.
Hence, God's final step in being our life is to make us His habitation, to make His home in us.

God will not make us individually His home. God has only
one home, not many homes. First Peter 2:5 says that the believers are living stones, not houses. A stone cannot become a
house by itself. Rather, many stones must be built together
in order to become a house. The spirit of every saved person
is God's habitation; God dwells in our spirit (1 Cor. 3:16). The
God who dwells in you also dwells in me and in every other
believer. The one God dwells in all of us. Hence, His habitation
is formed by our being built together (Eph. 2:22).

We can use electrical lamps as an illustration. Suppose we

have twenty lamps, and every lamp has electricity. There is only one electrical current; hence, the lamps do not have their own electricity. There can be dozens of electric lamps, but there will be only one electrical current in them. In the same way, although there are many believers, there is only one God in us. This God is the one Spirit, the one Lord, and the one Father (Eph. 4:4-6). The Father is in the Son, the Son has become the Spirit, and the Spirit dwells in our spirit.

When we deny ourselves, take God as life, live by Him, and let Him make home in our hearts, we will not be divided; instead, we will be one, because we will have God as our oneness. If after we are saved, we still live by our natural life and do not take God as life, we will not be one. If there is no oneness among us, we will not be the church. There will be many believers but not a built-up church. When every saint learns to deny himself and let God make His home in him, we will come together in oneness. There will be no you and no me; there will only be God. Only then will God be able to make His home in us.

THE CHURCH BEING BUILT
WHEN GOD MAKES HIS HOME IN US

Those in whom God can make His home, who let Him make His home in them, are being built up by God in the church. Such ones are not in themselves; they are in God, and God is the factor of their oneness. This oneness is the building, the church.

In 1 Corinthians 12 Paul speaks of the church as the Body. Verse 12 says, "Even as the body is one and has many members, yet all the members of the body, being many, are one body, so also is the Christ." This verse does not say, "So also is the church" but "so also is the Christ." The Body is constituted with many members and is not only the church. The Body is the Christ, because Christ is expressed through the members. These members do not live in their soul-life but in the divine life; they do not live by themselves but by Christ. Hence, when these members are joined together, they express Christ.

Our physical body has many members but only one life. Our physical life cannot be divided. The life in our hands exists at the same time in our feet, and the life in our ears exists simultaneously in our eyes. All our members have the same life. Our members can be coordinated and fitly joined to be one body because they have the same life. If one member does not have this life, it must be detached from our body. Similarly, the church is expressed through all the members taking Christ as life practically. If two brothers live in Christ, take Him as life, and let Him make His home in them, they will be blended together and will become one. Christ can make His home in us simultaneously, because we live in Him and are being delivered from ourselves; thus, there is a oneness among us. This oneness is the Lord, and it is also the church.

THE TWO SIGNIFICANCES
OF BREAKING BREAD

There are two significances to our breaking bread. The first significance is that when we break bread, we remember and enjoy the Lord. The bread signifies the Lord's body, which was broken for us on the cross, and the cup signifies His blood, which was shed for us on the cross (Matt. 26:26-28; Luke 22:19-20; 1 Cor. 11:23-26). When we break bread, we receive the bread and the cup. This indicates that we receive the Lord again. Our receiving and enjoying Him in this way is our remembrance of Him. The first significance of breaking the bread emphasizes our relationship with the Lord.

The second significance of breaking bread emphasizes our relationship with the saints. The bread that we break refers not only to the Lord's physical body but also to His mystical Body, which He gained in the Holy Spirit through His death and resurrection (10:16-17). The Lord Jesus gave up His physical body on the cross, and after His resurrection He gained His mystical Body in the Holy Spirit. The physical body that He gave on the cross was small, but the mystical Body that He gained in resurrection is large. The body that He gave was physical and had flesh and blood, but the Body that He gained is mystical and spiritual. The Body that He gained is comprised of all the believers throughout the ages. These are the two significances of our breaking bread.

When we break bread, we not only receive the Lord, enjoy

Him, and remember Him, but we also contact the saints, fellowship with them, and enjoy them. When we break bread, we enjoy not only the Lord but also the saints. We can read the Bible by ourselves, and we can pray by ourselves, but we cannot break the bread by ourselves. In order to break bread, there should be at least three to five saints. This is the principle of the Body.

Among God's children there is the concept of remembering the Lord when breaking bread, but they break bread while neglecting the mutual fellowship and enjoyment. The saints who criticize others and have unresolved problems yet break bread on the Lord's Day only remember the Lord; they do not have fellowship with the other members. Such bread-breaking cannot be considered as genuine. For this reason, the apostle Paul rebuked the Corinthians believers. Even though they ate the bread, there were divisions among them; hence, they were not eating the Lord's supper, and this offended the Lord (11:17-22). When we come together to break bread, we must deal with ourselves thoroughly before the Lord. We cannot criticize the saints or the church, on the one hand, yet break the bread, on the other. We must deal with such a situation.

THERE BEING NO REALITY OF THE CHURCH
WITHOUT GOD AS OUR LIFE

The Lord cannot make His home in us if we continue to live by ourselves and in ourselves. When we are occupied with ourselves, He does not have the ground to make home in us. As a result, we remain independent. In such a situation there is the church in name but not the church in reality. In other words, we will not have the reality of the church.

In order to have the reality of the church, every believer needs to live in Christ and let Christ make home in him in order to be delivered from the self. Then instead of despising, belittling, criticizing, or attacking one another, they will be in harmony. Furthermore, oneness will spontaneously be expressed among them, and all the saints will be one in God. If this is our situation, we will have the reality of the church, which is the built-up church. We will be a group of people who let Christ possess us and make home in us, and we will be living stones built together into God's habitation.

The building begins when our inner being becomes God's habitation, that is, when He can make His home in us. If God cannot make home in us, the building up of the church is not among us. At best, we are stones that have not been built into a spiritual house. If God has not made His home in us, we cannot have a part in the church as His practical habitation.

However, we should not say that a believer who does not let God make home in him is not in the church. Once a person is saved, he is in the church. However, practically speaking, the church is God's habitation, His spiritual temple and home, His dwelling place (1 Tim. 3:15). If we do not let Christ make home in us, we will not have the reality of the church. We should consider our situation. Can God make His home in us? Does He have ground in us? Does He occupy us? Are we practically in the church if we are full of criticism, judgment, despising, or disregard for the church? And are we practically in the church if we are dissatisfied, always complaining, and not in harmony with other believers? If this is our situation, we have not been built up into a house. Although we belong to the church, we have not been built into the church; we are detached from the church.

In order for the reality of the church to be expressed, there must be a situation where the saints genuinely learn in their practical living and in all things to deny themselves and to not live by themselves but to let God live in them and occupy them. Then they will be the reality of the church. Their inner being will be God's habitation; He will make home in them, and they will be filled unto all the fullness of God (Eph. 3:17a, 19b). Such a group of people will be in harmony and in one accord, and they will be in oneness, which is God Himself. They will be built up by the Lord, and they will be the church. When they come together, they will be the reality of the church.

GROWING IN LIFE
FOR THE BUILDING UP OF THE CHURCH

If we do not grow in life, that is, learn to take God as life, there will not be a way for us to be built up. Some saints have

remained in the same condition for twenty years. Their disposition and temperament have not been broken, and they do
not know what it is to live in God or to take God as life. For
this reason, they have not grown, the measure of the stature of
Christ has not increased in them, and they cannot be built up.

First Corinthians 3:9 says, "You are God's cultivated land,
God's building." This indicates that, on one hand, we are God's
building, and on the other hand, we are His cultivated land.
The expression *cultivated land* in the original language refers
to a farm for growing crops or produce. Just as a house needs to
be built, crops need to grow. We must grow in order to be built
up. In other words, if we do not grow in life, the church cannot
be built up.

When we grow in the divine life, we decrease and Christ
increases (John 3:30); that is, we become less and Christ becomes more. We are delivered from ourselves, and Christ gains
more ground to live in us. This is the meaning of growing. If we
would daily grow in such a way, the church will be built up practically and daily. Then God will have a dwelling place, which is
His home. When God's children come to this place, they will
say, "This is where we should be. We have come home because
here we have the object of our longing. We were thirsty, but now
we have living water. We were hungry, but now we have food.
We were homeless, wandering about, but here we have rest."
This is the situation in the church, the house of God.

THE CHURCH BEING THE PRIESTHOOD

The church is not only a spiritual temple, a spiritual house;
it is also a priesthood (1 Pet. 2:5). In the Old Testament the
priests were a group of people, and God's habitation was the
tabernacle and later the temple. The priests and God's habitation were separate. In the New Testament, however, God's dwelling place is His priests; the priests are His dwelling place. The
two—the priests and the habitation—have become one. However, the New Testament priests are not scattered individuals;
they are a corporate entity. The priests have been built up into
a corporate entity that serves God together.

The genuine service rendered to God is not individualistic. Rather, it is a coordinated service by those who are joined

together, one, and corporate. Such oneness, such joining together, is not arranged or organized by man. Genuine service involves learning not to live in ourselves but to let Christ be our life and to let Him occupy us and make His home in us so that we may be built up as a spiritual dwelling place. This is the way to become the priesthood. We are God's habitation for His dwelling place, and we are a priesthood for our service to God. The priesthood is a body of priests who are coordinated together and who serve God. This coordination is living and in life; it is full of the measure of life and the element of life. Such a service supplies others with the fullness of life.

The issue of God being life in us is that we are built up to become the habitation of God. Such a habitation is a spiritual temple and also a priesthood. This is where God can make His home, and it is where He is served. On one hand, we express God; on the other hand, we serve Him. This is the glorious result of taking God as life.

CHAPTER FOURTEEN

THE CHURCH BEING OUR LIVING

Scripture Reading: Rom. 12:5; 1 Tim. 3:15

In the previous two chapters we saw that the corporate aspect of the experience of God as life is for the building up of the church. In this chapter we will have practical fellowship concerning the church as our living.

THE CHURCH BEING OUR HOUSEHOLD

As believers, we must be clear that the church is God's home and also our household and dwelling place (1 Tim. 3:15; Eph. 2:19, 22). Every proper person is born into a family. Not only so, as soon as a person is born, he is a member of a household. Children who are born without a dwelling place are very pitiful. Hence, it is not enough for a person to have parents; he must also have a dwelling place. This applies not only to the physical realm but also to the spiritual realm. When we were regenerated, we were born of God's household and in God's dwelling place. As soon as we were born spiritually, the church became our household and dwelling place.

It is regrettable that among today's Christians, many were not saved into the practical church life. They are like babies who are born outside of a household and are without a dwelling place. Many Christians find the church as their dwelling place only after a period of time; however, some remain homeless to the end. This is pitiful.

Spiritually speaking, I was like a child born by the wayside of a road, and I grew up in a dilapidated house. After a long time I gradually discovered that I was without a proper dwelling place. I could not find my spiritual home. I went to many Christian meetings and seriously observed the situation. After careful observation, I felt that none of them could be my dwelling place. Eventually, God raised up a meeting, and I felt that it was where I belonged. All my inward needs were satisfied there. That was when I found my spiritual home.

EVERYTHING IN THE CHURCH BEING CHRIST

Perhaps someone would ask why the many groups in Christianity are not our home. Let me use an example. My surname is Lee, and my genealogy and bloodline belong to the Lee family. Thus, I belong to the Lee family. I cannot say that the Chang family is my family. Similarly, as regenerated believers, we belong to Christ, and our genealogy is Christ. Thus, we cannot find our home with a group that does not belong to Christ or does not proceed from His genealogy. A genuine church must belong to Christ; it allows Him to live in it. In God's house the clothes we wear are Christ, the water we drink is Christ, and the food we eat is also Christ. Everything in the church is Christ.

Apart from Christ, there cannot be anything else in the church. If in any aspect of the church Christ is replaced with something else, whether it be in genealogy, ground, truth, or life, we will no longer be the church. The genealogy of the church is Christ, the ground of the church is Christ, the content of the church is Christ, and the appearance of the church is also Christ; everything related to the church is Christ. The life supply in the church as our home is also Christ. This is a matter of our eating and drinking. Our living is also Christ. This is a matter of our expression. Hence, everything in the church is Christ. Suppose a group of Christians calls itself the church, but its genealogy, ground, life supply, and living are not Christ. We should question whether it is the church. If a church is genuine, everything should be Christ.

Hence, we should rejoice because we were born in the church. Here the genealogy, ground, and supply are Christ, and being the church requires that our living be Christ. The church gives us Christ, and we should express Christ in our living. Everything must be Christ. We were born of this place, and we live in this place. We are blessed because we have a home.

CHRIST BEING OUR LIFE AND
THE CHURCH BEING OUR LIVING

The church is a great topic. Ephesians 5:32 says, "This mystery is great, but I speak with regard to Christ and the church." The great mystery in the universe is Christ and the church. Christ and the church are our vision and our light. Our vision is not heaven and hell, forgiveness of sins, receiving salvation, or being delivered from eternal perdition. Our vision is Christ and the church. Hence, Christ and the church are the only goal of our labor and work, which begins with leading people to salvation with the gospel and includes edifying and perfecting the saints. Christ is our life, and the church is our living. Christ is in us to be our life, and His living out from us as our living is the church. In other words, Christ is our life within and our living without. When He is expressed through us outwardly, He becomes our living, and this is the church.

We have given many messages concerning letting Christ be our life and letting Him live in us; our unique desire is to let Christ live out from us. When Christ is lived out from us, we are the church. When He is expressed in our living, He and the church are one. Hence, Christ is our life, and the church is our living. The two are the great mystery. Every believer has the divine life. Although we are many, we have the same life— Christ. As believers, we also have a living, which is the expression of the divine life within us. It may seem as though we each have our own living. However, since we share the same life, we also share the same living (Rom. 12:5). This living is the church, which is the corporate Christ, that is, the corporate expression of the lived-out Christ.

In the book of Acts the living of the early believers was altogether corporate, not individualistic. Peter did not have a living, John another living, and James yet another living. They had the same living. Not only did they share the same divine life, but they also shared the same living, which is the church. Within they had Christ, and without they had the church. Within they had Christ living, and without they lived in the church. The Christ whom they lived out was their corporate living. Such a corporate living is the church. Just as Christ was their common life inwardly, so also the church was their common living outwardly.

CHRISTIAN LIVING NOT BEING SEPARATE
FROM THE CHURCH

Although Christians can worship God individually, such worship is small and light; it is not weighty. For worship to be weighty, it must be the worship of saints gathered together. Likewise, the individual aspect of our service to God is light. Proper Christian service is corporate. We must serve together with other brothers and sisters in order for our service to be weighty. This is also true of our spiritual pursuit and spiritual life. Being delivered from sin, overcoming the world, being sanctified, and living for the Lord seem to be matters for individual pursuit. However, the more we pursue them individually, the more we fail to obtain them. In order to experience genuine overcoming, sanctification, and spirituality, we must pursue with the brothers and sisters. This is according to 2 Timothy 2:22, which says, "Pursue...with those who call on the Lord out of a pure heart." Hence, even our spiritual life and spiritual pursuit should be corporate, not individualistic. This does not annul the individual aspect of the Christian life; rather, it means that our individual pursuit will be firm only when it is for the corporate pursuit.

In conclusion, in order to be a Christian, we must live in the church; we cannot be separated from the church. This is similar to the fact that a person cannot be separated from his home; he must live in a home. When he loses his home, he will become a pitiful and abnormal person without rest and warmth. In the same principle, we as Christians need a home, which is the church. If we are separated from the church, we are pitiful and abnormal Christians.

CHRISTIAN LIVING BEING ATTACHED TO THE CHURCH

The more a person fellowships with the Lord and lives in Him, taking Him as life and expressing Him, the less likely he is to be separated from the church. The more proper a person is, the less likely he is to be separated from his home. If he keeps things from his family, he is not a proper person but instead has a problem. A proper child will always tell his family every-thing pertaining to himself, whether or not it is significant, and he will always be attached to his family. In the same prin-ciple, everything pertaining to a proper Christian is related to the church. There are problems whenever a Christian is unwill-ing to let the church know his situation.

For example, if a student passes the entrance exam to a school but does not want to let the church know, then there must be something improper concerning that school. If a brother finds a job but is afraid to let the church know, then there must be something wrong with the job. When some young saints have secret friendships and do not let the saints in the church know, then there must be something wrong in their relation-ship. Hence, anything in our living or conduct that we are afraid to let the church know about or that cannot be related to the church is a problem and is not proper. Anything that we do apart from the church or without the knowledge of the church must be inappropriate.

This does not mean that we do not have any personal free-dom. Everyone has personal freedom and privacy, which should not be violated. However, privacy is one thing, and hiding some-thing from the church is another thing. We must understand the difference between privacy and a work in darkness. For example, I do not tell others how much money I have in my pocket, because this is a personal matter before God; it is not public. However, it is not a dark secret, nor is it something that I am afraid to let others know. If asked, I have nothing to fear in letting someone know. If the money in my possession had a suspicious source, it would not be something that I would want to fellowship about with the saints. It would be something in darkness, not in the light. It would also make me improper. Hence, in principle we should be able to let the church know everything related to our living and our walk.

KEEPING ORDER IN THE CHURCH

There is order in the church life. There are parents and sib-lings in a family, and there is no confusion when each person maintains this order. For example, Brother Lin is neither the father nor the mother in his family. He has a younger brother and a younger sister as well as an older sister. Hence, he knows his place in his family. He knows who is above and who is below him. This is very clear. As another example, a family may have many naughty children who often quarrel among themselves. However, when something happens, they know what is the proper order. This is a normal situation in a family, and this is also the situation in the church. Brother Lin would probably say that in the big family of the church he is not the father, nor the mother, nor the oldest brother, nor the second oldest. He might say that he is the youngest. Such a reply is too humble, because in the church there will always be some who are younger. If Brother Lin has been saved for a year, those who have been saved for a month are his younger siblings.

This example shows that the church resembles the situation of a family, in which everyone keeps the order and knows his place. In some families the oldest son may be thirty years old, and his youngest sibling is only seven or eight years old. The oldest son is like a father to his younger siblings. This is also the situation in the church. A certain brother may be rather experienced in the Lord and is therefore more like a father than a brother to the others. Some sisters are rather experienced and are qualified not only to be an older sister but even a mother. We should respect such ones. Those who are clear concerning this matter will receive the greatest benefit in the church.

In this present age there is an undesirable trend, especially among the young people, that emphasizes equality and democracy. According to this trend, there should be equality and freedom within every social group. This is a dreadful thing. Suppose the youngest child insists on equality and democracy and says, "This is the twentieth century. We should have equality in our home. Even though you are our father, you are the same as the rest of us. We should all stand on equal footing and practice democracy in everything. We should have a meeting and make decisions by voting." Would this be a family? In a family we should learn to love one another, and there should be mutual care, compassion, and warmth. However, there is also order in a family. There is a father and a mother, there are older brothers and sisters, and there are younger brothers and sisters. Even though they love one another, they must still keep the order in the family. The proper situation in a family includes order. This is also the proper situation in the church.

It would be dreadful for someone to say, "We are all saved and belong to the Lord. We are brothers and sisters in Him; hence, we should be equal and democratic in the church. In every matter we should have a meeting and vote." As the house of God, the church should not be like this. In the church of God there is order. We all belong to the Lord and should have care, compassion, and warmth for one another, but this does not annul the order in God's house. First Peter 5:5 says, "Younger men, be subject to elders." This word proves that in God's house there is a distinction between older saints and younger saints. There is harmony when the order is kept in a family.

If four or five saints want to preach the gospel in a suburb, can they keep the order and know whom to listen to? It would be a beautiful sight if they keep the order such that the younger ones listen to the older ones. In contrast, if they are in confusion because everyone is striving to be equal and democratic, they will not express the church. The church is full of Christ with love, compassion, and warmth, but the church is also full of authority and order.

Our authority is not the pope. Our authority is Christ the Head expressed in every member. Every member has the authority of the Head, which is the order ordained by the Head. This order is based on our measure of the stature of Christ. If a brother has a greater measure of the stature of Christ, is more mature in life, and more experienced in the Lord, he is an older brother and bears authority. If he does not express a measure of the stature of Christ, is not mature in the divine life, and is not experienced in the Lord, he is a younger brother and should be subject to authority. Hence, no one is the authority; rather, we should all bear the authority of the Head, and we should also be subject to one another.

LOVING THE CHURCH
AND NOT CRITICIZING THE SAINTS

We must learn to treasure our household and to love all the members. We should not criticize or despise one another, nor should we discuss the shortcomings of our family members to outsiders. Such improper behavior will not be blessed. Let us consider our own families in the flesh. Even though we may see the mistakes of our parents or our siblings, we should not criticize them carelessly. This does not mean that I should be sent to the police station if I criticize someone. Rather, this means that since I treasure my family, respect my parents, and love my siblings, I will not criticize their mistakes, much less speak ill of them to others.

It is regrettable that one can encounter criticism, judgment, and despising in many Christian groups. A person who criticizes his parents or his siblings will not only have problems in his family but will also damage his family. Once a family suffers damage, the members also suffer a loss. Therefore, instead of criticizing or despising, we should find a proper way to render help in love.

The proper way to render help is to pray. If there is an appropriate opportunity to contact a member, we should stand in the proper position and speak. This is not to rebuke him but to admonish him. When parents make a mistake, the children can speak a few words to them, but not to condemn, despise, criticize, or judge them. Suppose an older brother or sister transgresses or offends another member, and a younger saint witnesses it. The younger saint will not be blessed if he criticizes, judges, or gossips concerning what he saw. He should bring the matter before the Lord in prayer and look for an appropriate opportunity to speak in a proper way and with the attitude and spirit of an instructed one. When the older saint is delivered, the church will also be delivered, and the younger saint will be delivered as well. This will preserve the church and give grace to all the members.

FULFILLING OBLIGATIONS IN THE CHURCH

The church is our household and dwelling place, in which we are not without obligations. This means that we should fulfill our part to love, support, and strengthen the church. We should not regard the church as belonging to someone else. The church belongs to all the saints. We must care for the church, just as we care for our own household. For example, if we see a "broken window" in the church as our dwelling place, we should tell a responsible brother, just as we would tell our parents or older siblings if there were a broken window in our home. If a "broken window" is not a concern to us, we are like an outsider. We have obligations and responsibilities in the church as our home.

HAVING ACTIVITIES IN THE CHURCH

Since the church is our home, we must function and serve in the church. In the prayer meeting we should learn to receive the burden and pray for the matters of the church. In the bread-breaking meeting we should learn to worship with all the saints. According to the Lord's leading and the strength that He gives us, we should participate in all the activities of the church, including gospel activities and shepherding the saints.

In conclusion, we should live in the church. We should learn to recognize our place, be subject to the authority of the church, fulfill our obligations, and function according to our portion. We should also learn to fellowship with the saints. This is the church life; this is the life of Christ living in us and being lived out of us.